Managing Editor
Mara Ellen Guckian

Editor in Chief
Karen J. Goldfluss, M.S. Ed.

Creative Director
Sarah M. Smith

Illustrator
Clint McKnight

Cover Artist
Barb Lorseyedi

Art Coordinator
Renée Mc Elwee

Imaging
James Edward Grace
Craig Gunnell

Publisher
Mary D. Smith, M.S. Ed.

GRADE

Critical Thinking
Test-taking Practice for
READING

TCR 3912

D1408205

STUDENTS WILL:
- Improve reading skills
- Gain critical-thinking skills
- Develop effective strategies to answer questions
- Become more confident test takers

Teacher Created Resources

Author
Julia McMeans, M.Ed.

CORRELATED TO COMMON CORE STANDARDS

For correlations to the Common Core State Standards, see pages 10–11. Correlations can also be found at *http://www.teachercreated.com/standards.*

Teacher Created Resources
6421 Industry Way
Westminster, CA 92683
www.teachercreated.com
ISBN: 978-1-4206-3912-4

© 2014 Teacher Created Resources
Made in U.S.A.

Teacher Created Resources

Table of Contents

Introduction

So here we are, well into the new millennium and still no robotic classroom assistant who grades all the papers and makes sure that no one in the back of the room is talking; still no time-travel phone booth that allows us to take our class on a trip to Independence Hall, circa 1776; and still no brain-scanning technology that instantly assesses the reading-comprehension skills of our students.

Here are the facts: Contemporary educators assess students in basically the same ways they were assessed fifty years ago—students read a passage and then they answer a question like this:

1. Why do you think the author is using humor to introduce the topic of test-taking to her audience?

 A. The author is trying to trick the reader into thinking this is a joke book.

 B. The author does not think test-taking is very important.

 C. The author has invented a brain-scanning device.

 D. The author is trying to use humor to introduce a stressful topic.

The answer is D. Standardized testing, whether you are the test-giver or the test-taker, is a high-stakes, stressful proposition, and for the time being there's no getting away from all those tiny bubbles! So let's breathe deeply and try to figure out the most effective ways in which to help our students fill in all those tiny bubbles correctly!

Much has been written about test-taking strategies, most of it focused on the actual techniques that students can use to help navigate multiple-choice questions. While we acknowledge the necessity of that skill set, the focus of these books is somewhat different.

This book concentrates on the requisite reading-comprehension skills that are prevalent on standardized multiple-choice tests and the ways in which we can teach students to first recognize the type of questions they are being asked, and second use the most effective strategies to answer specific types of reading-comprehension questions.

We believe that if students have an awareness, a kind of metacognition, about the specific skills that are evaluated and an ability to discriminate among the array of questions they are being asked, then they will become more confident and effective test-takers.

Explicit and Implicit Questions

Reading-comprehension tests primarily ask two types of overarching questions. These questions are either *explicit* or *implicit*.

Explicit Questions

Explicit questions are questions for which there is a literal, easy-to-find answer. These kinds of questions are also called "right there" questions, because students can find the answer stated overtly right there in the text.

- Explicit questions often begin with the words: *who*, *what*, *when*, or *where*.

- Explicit questions fall under the Bloom's Taxonomy category of *Remembering* (also known as *Knowledge*), requiring students to simply recall or locate information.

- Explicit questions are often the easiest reading-comprehension questions for students to answer.

Remember, to answer an explicit question, look for the answer written *right there* in the text. Locate it and point right to it!

Implicit Questions

Implicit questions are questions that require the reader to read between the lines to identify information that is often not stated literally but is implied by the text.

- Implicit questions require students to draw conclusions and to make deductions and predictions.

- Implicit questions frequently require that students make text-to-self and text-to-world connections.

- Implicit questions fall under the Bloom's Taxonomy category of *Analyzing and Evaluating*, which requires students to make judgments, compare and contrast, and distinguish between facts and opinions.

- Implicit questions are often extremely challenging for students to answer.

To answer an implicit question, use clues from the story plus your own experience. Implicit questions often begin with the word *why*.

Making Inferences and Drawing Conclusions

Drawing a conclusion based on implied information in a text is a skill that requires practice. In order to draw a reasonable conclusion and answer an inferential question, the reader must identify the unstated or implied information in a text, and then combine it with his or her own experiences and knowledge of the world (prior knowledge).

Use the "Boy in the Pond" activity on pages 7–9 to help students discriminate between implicit and explicit questions.

Explicit and Implicit Questions *(cont.)*

Directions: Look at the cartoon. What do you think is happening in this picture? Answer these questions.

1. Why are the dog and cat pointing at each other?

2. Why is the fish laughing?

3. Why is the bird relaxing in a hammock?

4. Why aren't the fish and the bird pointing at each other or at the cat or the dog?

5. Will the bird or the fish get blamed for what has happened? Why or why not?

Explicit and Implicit Questions *(cont.)*

Directions: Look at the cartoon. Would you like to be friends with the tortoise? Why or why not?

"Boy in the Pond" Questions

Directions: Use the illustration on the next page to help you answer these questions. Put an **I** on the shortline after any *implicit* questions. Put an **E** on the shortline after any *explicit* questions. Answer the questions on the longer lines.

1. Is the boy in the water? _____

_____

2. What season is it? _____

_____

3. Is the tree branch broken? _____

_____

4. If the boy crawled out of the water, would the goat butt him? _____

_____

5. Is a goat standing by the pond? _____

_____

6. Will the branch fall on the boy's head? _____

_____

7. How did the boy get into the water? _____

_____

8. Why doesn't the tree have any leaves? _____

_____

9. If it rains, will leaves grow on the tree? _____

_____

10. Will the boy get into trouble? _____

_____

"Boy in the Pond" Illustration

Directions: Look at the picture. Use the illustration to answer the questions on the previous page.

"Boy in the Pond" Explanation

Below you will find a detailed explanation regarding the *implicit* or *explicit* nature of each question.

1. Is the boy in the water? _____E_____

This is an explicit question because we can see the boy in the water.

2. What season is it? _____I_____

This is an implicit question. The season (spring or summer) is hinted at by the leaves on the deciduous tree, the attire of the boy, and the recreational activity he is engaged in.

3. Is the tree branch broken? _____E_____

This is an explicit question because we can see the broken branch.

4. If the boy crawled out of the water, would the goat butt him? _____I_____

This is an implicit question. The viewer has to combine clues from the picture of the goat standing next to the pond and prior knowledge that goats often *do* butt people to arrive at a reasonable answer.

5. Is a goat standing by the pond? _____E_____

This is an explicit question because we can see the goat standing by the pond.

6. Will the branch fall on the boy's head? _____I_____

This is an implicit question. The picture suggests that the branch will fall on the boy's head because it is broken and in the process of falling, and the boy is standing directly beneath it.

7. How did the boy get into the water? _____I_____

This is an implicit question. It is implied that the boy was on the branch, that it broke, and that he fell into the water.

8. Why doesn't the tree have any leaves? _____I_____

This is an implicit question because the reason is implied by picture clues. The viewer can deduce that it is spring or summer because there are leaves on nearby trees and grass growing around the pond. The tree in question has no leaves and has brittle branches. Students will have to draw on personal knowledge regarding what it means when a tree has no leaves in the growing season.

9. Will leaves grow on the tree if it rains? _____I_____

This is an implicit question. It is implied that the tree is dead. (See explanation for #8.) Therefore, no amount of rain will make a dead tree sprout leaves.

10. Do you think the boy will get into trouble? _____I_____

This is an implicit question. We do not see the boy getting into trouble. The viewer has to use picture clues (The boy did something dangerous.) and draw on personal experience (Have I ever gotten into trouble for doing something dangerous?) to answer the question.

Common Core State Standards Correlation

Each passage and question in *Critical Thinking: Test-taking Practice for Reading (Grade 3)* meets one or more of the following Common Core State Standards © Copyright 2010. National Governors Association Center for Best Practices and Council of Chief State School Officers. All rights reserved. For more information about these standards, go to *http://www.corestandards.org/* or *http://teachercreated.com/standards*.

Reading: Literature	Page Correlations
Key Ideas and Details	
ELA.RL.3.1 Ask and answer questions to demonstrate understanding of a text, referring explicitly to the text as the basis for the answers.	18-22, 23-26, 44-46, 51-56, 72-74
ELA.RL.3.2 Recount stories, including fables, folktales, and myths from diverse cultures; determine the central message, lesson, or moral and explain how it is conveyed through key details in the text.	18-22, 23-26, 44-46, 51-56
ELA.RL.3.3 Describe characters in a story (e.g., their traits, motivations, or feelings) and explain how their actions contribute to the sequence of events.	18-22, 23-26, 44-46, 51-56, 72-74
Craft and Structure	
ELA.RL.3.4 Determine the meaning of words and phrases as they are used in a text, distinguishing literal from nonliteral language.	44-46, 72-74
ELA.RL.3.5 Refer to parts of stories, dramas, and poems when writing or speaking about a text, using terms such as chapter, scene, and stanza; describe how each successive part builds on earlier sections.	44-46
ELA.RL.3.6 Distinguish their own point of view from that of the narrator or those of the characters.	51-56
Range of Reading and Level of Text Complexity	
ELA.RL.3.10 By the end of the year, read and comprehend literature, including stories, dramas, and poetry, at the high end of the grades 2–3 text complexity band independently and proficiently.	all passages
Reading: Informational Text	
Key Ideas and Details	
ELA.RI.3.1 Ask and answer questions to demonstrate understanding of a text, referring explicitly to the text as the basis for the answers.	27-29, 30-33, 34-37, 38-43, 47-50, 57-60, 61-64, 65-68, 69-71, 75-77
ELA.RI.3.2 Determine the main idea of a text; recount the key details and explain how they support the main idea.	27-29, 30-33, 38-43, 75-77
ELA.RI.3.3 Describe the relationship between a series of historical events, scientific ideas or concepts, or steps in technical procedures in a text, using language that pertains to time, sequence, and cause/effect.	27-29, 34-37, 38-43, 47-50, 57-60, 61-64, 65-68, 69-71, 75-77

Handwritten margin notes (left side): Qtr– ; 1,2,4 ; 1,4 ; 2, ; 1 ; 2,4 ; 2,4 ; 1,4 ; 1(2)3 ; 1,4 ; 3

Common Core State Standards Correlation *(cont.)*

Reading: Informational Text *(cont.)*	
Craft and Structure	**Page Correlations**
ELA.RI.3.4 Determine the meaning of general academic and domain–specific words and phrases in a text relevant to a *grade 3 topic or subject area*.	30-33, 34-37, 38-43, 47-50, 57-60, 61-64, 65-68
ELA.RI.3.5 Use text features and search tools (e.g., key words, side bars, hyperlinks) to locate information relevant to a given topic efficiently.	18-22, 27-29, 30-33, 38-43
ELA.RI.3.6 Distinguish their own point of view from that of the author of a text.	30-33
Integration of Knowledge and Ideas	
ELA.RI.3.7 Use information gained from illustrations (e.g. maps, photographs) and the words in a text to demonstrate understanding of the text (e.g. where, when, why, and how key events occur).	30-33, 38-43, 57-60
ELA.RI.3.8 Describe the logical connection between particular sentences and paragraphs in a text (e.g., comparison, cause/effect, first/second/third in a sequence).	30-33, 57-60, 61-64, 69-71, 75-77
Range of Reading and Level of Text Complexity	
ELA.RI.3.10 By the end of the year, read and comprehend informational texts, including history/social studies, science, and technical texts, at the high end of the grades 2–3 text complexity band independently and proficiently.	all passages

Reading: Foundational Skills	
Phonics and Word Recognition	
ELA.RF.3.3 Know and apply grade-level phonics and word analysis skills in decoding words.	all passages
Fluency	
ELA.RF.3.4 Read with sufficient accuracy and fluency to support comprehension.	all passages

Language	
Vocabulary Acquisition and Use	
ELA.L.3.4 Determine or clarify the meaning of unknown and multiple–meaning words and phrases based on grade 3 reading and content, choosing flexibly from a range of strategies.	30-33, 34-37, 38-43, 57-60, 61-64, 65-68
ELA.L.3.5 Demonstrate understanding of figurative language, word relationships and nuances in word meanings.	18-22, 38-43, 44-46, 47-50
ELA.L.3.6 Acquire and use accurately grade–appropriate conversational, general academic, and domain–specific words and phrases, including those that signal spatial and temporal relationships (e.g., *After dinner that night we went looking for them).*	18-22, 23-26, 72-74, 75-77

Process Skills

Reading-comprehension tests assess student ability in two main areas: decoding and deriving meaning. Students can expect to encounter questions that cover all of the areas outlined below on standardized assessments.

Vocabulary

Vocabulary questions on reading-comprehension tests typically ask students to identify and determine the meaning of words and word parts by employing a variety of strategies, including the following:

- Identifying synonyms, antonyms, homophones, and multiple-meaning words
- Identifying the meaning of words using prefixes and suffixes
- Using reference materials: dictionary, thesaurus, and glossary
- Using root words and word origins
- Using context clues: definition, contrast, restatement, and inference

Fiction

Reading-comprehension tests usually ask students to analyze, interpret, and/or identify the following elements of fiction:

- Characters, including their *traits, feelings, beliefs, motives,* and *actions*
- Literary devices and figurative language, including *hyperbole, metaphor, analogy, anthropomorphism, alliteration, simile, personification, onomatopoeia,* and *idioms*
- Literary elements, including *plot, setting,* and *theme*
- Poetry, including *rhyme, rhythm, stanza, verse,* and *meter*
- Genres and their characteristics, *including folk* and *fairy tales, fiction, myths, poems, fables, fantasies, historical fiction,* and *chapter books*

Nonfiction

Reading-comprehension tests ask students to analyze and deconstruct the following elements of nonfiction passages:

- Text structure, including *compare and contrast, chronological,* and *cause and effect*
- Author's purpose and point of view, including *identifying intent* and *bias*
- Graphic features including, *graphs, tables, charts,* etc.
- Sequence of events
- Main idea, supporting details, and extraneous information
- Details from the text that support ideas
- Distinction between fact and opinion, identifying fact or opinion
- Types of nonfiction and their characteristics, including *biographies* and *autobiographies*
- Summarizing a passage
- Paraphrasing the main idea

> **Remind students…**
> Explicit and implicit questions can be framed around many process skills. For example, there may be character-analysis questions that are both explicit and implicit.

Content References for Student Questions

Students can expect to find questions about the topics and skills listed below on reading-comprehension tests. This list may be used as a reference so that students are aware, in advance, of the types of questions they may be asked. Encourage students to review this list often. Room has been provided alongside the list for student notes. Ultimately, you never want students to be surprised by the type of questions that they are being asked.

Vocabulary

Decoding and Structural Analysis

- synonyms
- antonyms
- homophones
- multiple-meaning words
- prefixes
- suffixes
- root words
- word origins

Determining Meaning

- context clues
- definition
- compare and contrast
- restatement
- inference

Reference Materials

- dictionary
- thesaurus
- glossary

Nonfiction

Text Structure

- compare and contrast
- chronological order
- cause and effect

Author's Purpose

- point of view
- intent
- bias
- fact and opinion

Main Idea

- supporting details
- extraneous information
- paraphrasing and summarizing

Content References for Student Questions *(cont.)*

Fiction

Character Analysis

- traits
- feelings
- beliefs
- motives
- actions

Literary Devices and Figurative Language

- hyperbole
- metaphor
- analogy
- anthropomorphism
- alliteration
- simile
- personification
- onomatopoeia
- idioms

Literary Elements

- plot
  - —sequence of events
  - —main problem
  - —conflict and resolution
- setting
- theme

Poetry

- rhyme
- rhythm
- stanza
- verse
- meter

Characteristics of Genres

- folk and fairy tales
- fiction and nonfiction
- myths
- poems
- fables
- fantasies
- historical fiction
- biographies and autobiographies
- chapter books

How This Book Is Organized

This book is organized into three tests: Test A, Test B, and Test C. Each test has 50 questions and contains a mix of the types of questions discussed previously. The tests are scaffolded so that the degree of assistance provided decreases with each assessment.

Test A

Test A provides students with specific and detailed guidance regarding how to approach the passages and the test questions in the form of call-out boxes along the sides of both the passage and questions. The call-out boxes appear as rectangular-shaped boxes that are positioned beside relevant sections of text and questions. You will notice that students are asked to determine whether some of the questions are implicit or explicit. You may instruct students to indicate their responses by using either an **E** for *explicit*, or an **I** for *implicit*.

Example from Test A

Directions: Read the story called "The Big Snow." Then answer questions 12–22.

The Big Snow

Last year my family and I moved from Miami, Florida to Troy, Vermont. We moved because my mom got a new job at a hospital. My mom is a doctor. She's a heart doctor. She helps people who have diseases in their hearts.

When I found out that we were moving, I was scared. I had lived in Florida my whole life. All of my friends were there. It made me sad to think that I would be leaving them.

One day when I was talking to my dad about it, he said, "Hey, Chip, I can think of something good about moving to Vermont."

"What's that?" I asked.

"I'll give you a clue. It's cold and white!" my dad replied.

I had forgotten all about snow. It doesn't snow in Florida. The only snow I ever saw was in the movies or on television. Maybe moving wouldn't be so bad after all.

> Think about how the characters feel.

14. Why does Chip feel scared about moving?

 A. He is moving to a rough neighborhood.

 B. He is afraid of flying on an airplane.

 C. New things can often be scary.

 D. He is probably afraid of snow.

Type of Question: _____

> Imagine how you would feel if you had to move to a new place.

How This Book Is Organized *(cont.)*

Test B

Test B continues to provide call-out support, but there is less of it, and it is more general in nature.

Example from Test B

Directions: Read the story called "Three Swinging Pigs and a Wolf." Then answer questions 31–40.

Three Swinging Pigs and a Wolf

Once upon a time there lived three little pigs. They were called Pink, Dink, and Stink. Pink got his name because he was the pinkest pig that anyone had ever seen. He was the color of cotton candy. Dink was short for Dinky. Dink got his name because he was very small for his age. He was the runt of the litter. The runt is the smallest animal born. And Stink, well, you can pretty much guess how he got his name.

> What kind of story is this?

32. What is the relationship between the pigs?
    A. They are friends.
    B. They are brothers.
    C. They are neighbors.
    D. They are sisters.

> Look for story clues.

Test C

Test C also provides 50 practice questions but no call-out support. It is an opportunity for students to take a reading-comprehension assessment independently. This will give both you and your students an opportunity to see the degree to which they have internalized not only the ability to correctly identify question types, but also the specific strategies they can employ to answer the questions.

How This Book Is Organized (cont.)

Answer Key

The answer key at the back of this book was designed to be another teaching and learning tool for both teacher and students. While it's important for students to know which answer is correct, it is equally useful for students to understand why the other options are incorrect. This answer key provides the correct answers to the questions, identifies the types of questions being asked, and details why the other options are incorrect.

The sample below shows the answer to the question in the example for Test A on page 15. The answer key provides the correct answer, the specific type of question asked, and when appropriate, whether the question is *explicit* (E) or *implicit* (I). It also provides a brief explanation regarding the correct answer and information regarding why the other options are incorrect. A bubble answer sheet is also provided on page 78.

Sample Answer Key Response

14. Correct Answer: C *(Making Inferences)* **I**

Chip states that he was afraid and that he would miss his friends. Most people would feel scared if they were going to be in an unfamiliar situation with people they don't know.

Incorrect Answers:

A. There is nothing to suggest that Chip is moving to a rough neighborhood.

B. There is nothing to suggest that Chip is fearful of flying on a plane.

D. Chip is not afraid of snow; he is just unfamiliar with it.

Test A | Name: _____

Directions: Read the following chapters from *Robinson Crusoe (for Children)* by James Baldwin. Then answer questions 1–11.

Robinson Crusoe

Chapter 1: I Wish To Be a Sailor

My name is Robinson Crusoe. I was born in the old city of York, where there is a broad river, with ships coming and going.

When I was a little boy, I spent much of my time looking at the river. How pleasant was the quiet stream, flowing, always flowing toward the faraway sea! I liked to watch the ships as they came in with their white sails spread to the wind. I liked to think of the strange lands which they must have visited, and of the many wonderful things they must have passed.

I wished to be a sailor. I thought how grand it must be to sail and sail on the wide blue sea, with the sky above and the waves beneath. Nothing could be pleasanter.

My father wanted me to learn a trade, but I could not bear the thought of it. I could not bear the thought of working every day in a dusty shop.

I did not wish to stay in York all of my life. I wanted to see the world. I would be a sailor and nothing else.

My mother was very sad when I told her.

A sailor's life, she said, was a hard life. There were many storms at sea, and ships were often wrecked.

She told me, too, that there were great fishes in the sea, and that they would eat me up if I fell into the water.

Then she gave me a cake, and kissed me.

"How much safer is it to be at home!" she said.

But I would not listen to her. My mind was made up, and a sailor I would be. When I was eighteen years old, I left my pleasant home and went to sea.

Chapter 2: I Make My First Voyage

I soon found that my mother's words were true. A sailor's life is indeed a hard life.

There was no time for play on board our ship. Even in the fairest weather there was much work to be done.

> Take a quick look at the questions before you read the passage.

> Review the names of the chapters before you begin to read the passage.

Test A   Name: _____

Robinson Crusoe *(cont.)*

On the very first night the wind began to blow. The waves rolled high. The ship was tossed this way and that. Never had I seen such a storm.

All night long the wind blew. I was so badly frightened that I did not know what to do. I thought the ship would surely go to the bottom. Then I remembered my pleasant home and the words of my kind mother.

"If I live to reach dry land," I said to myself, "I will give up this thought of being a sailor. I will go home and stay with my father and mother. I will never set foot on another ship."

Day came. The storm was worse than before. I felt sure that we were lost. But toward evening the sky began to clear. The wind died away. The waves went down. The storm was over.

The next morning the sun rose bright and warm upon a smooth sea. It was a beautiful sight.

As I stood looking out over the wide water, the first mate came up. He was a kind man and always friendly to me.

> Who is telling this story?

"Well, Bob," he said, "how do you like it? Were you frightened by that little gale?"

"I hope you don't call it a little gale," I said. "Indeed it was a terrible storm."

The mate laughed.

"Do you call that a storm?" he asked. "Why, it was nothing at all. You are only a fresh-water sailor, Bob. Wait till we have a real storm."

And so I soon forgot my fears.

Little by little, I gave up all thoughts of going home again. "A sailor's life for me," I said.

My first voyage was not a long one.

I visited no new lands, for the ship went only to London. But the things which I saw in that great city seemed very wonderful to me.

Nothing would satisfy me but to make a long voyage. I wished to see the whole world.

> How does Robinson feel after the storm has passed?

Chapter 3: I See Much of the World

It was easy to find a ship of my liking; for all kinds of trading vessels go out from London to every country that is known.

One day I met an old sea captain who had often been to the coast of Africa. He was pleased with my talk.

Test A | Name: _____

Robinson Crusoe *(cont.)*

Chapter 3: I See Much of the World *(cont.)*

"If you want to see the world," he said, "you must sail with me."

And then he told me that he was going to Africa, to trade with the people there. He would carry out a load of goods to exchange for gold dust and feathers and other rare and curious things.

I was very glad to go with him. I would see strange lands and people different from me. I would have a stirring adventure.

Before ten days had passed, we were out on the great ocean. Our ship headed toward the south.

The captain was very kind to me. He taught me much that every sailor ought to know. He showed me how to steer and manage the vessel. He told me about the tides and the compass and how to reckon the ship's course.

> How do you think Robinson will change in the story?

The voyage was a pleasant one, and I saw more wonderful things than I can name.

When, at last, we sailed back to London, we had enough gold to make a poor man rich.

I had nearly six pounds of the yellow dust for my own share. I had learned to be a trader as well as a sailor.

It would take too long to tell you of all my voyages. Some of them were happy and successful; but most were unpleasant and full of disappointment.

Sometimes I went to Africa, sometimes to the new land of South America. But wherever I sailed I found the life of a sailor by no means easy.

I did not care so much now to see strange sights and visit unknown shores. I cared more for the money or the goods that I would get by trading.

At last a sudden end was put to all my sailing. And it is of this that I will now tell you.

Questions 1–11: Select the best answer.

1. Who is narrating this story?

    A. a sea captain

    B. Robinson Crusoe

    C. Robinson's mother

    D. a shipmate

> The narrator is the person telling the story.

Type of Question: _____

Test A   Name: _____

Robinson Crusoe *(cont.)*

2. Why did Robinson want to be a sailor?

   A. His father was a sailor.

   B. He knew he could become rich trading gold dust.

   C. He was forced to become a sailor.

   D. He liked to watch ships come and go in the city he grew up in.

> Implicit questions often begin with "why."

Type of Question: _____

3. How did Robinson feel about learning a trade?

   A. angry

   B. bored

   C. safe

   D. excited

> What does Robinson say about learning a trade?

4. Why doesn't Robinson's mother want him to become a sailor?

   A. Because he won't earn that much money.

   B. Because he might get bored.

   C. Because he might get hurt.

   D. Because he might not learn a trade.

> Think of how your parents would feel if you went off to sea.

5. How old was Robinson when he set sail for the first time?

   A. 18

   B. 81

   C. 21

   D. 16

> Point Right To It!

Type of Question: _____

6. In what chapter does Robinson experience his first storm at sea?

   A. Chapter 1

   B. Chapter 2

   C. Chapter 3

   D. Chapters 2 and 3

> Use the chapter names to help you locate the information.

| Test A | Name: _____ |

Robinson Crusoe *(cont.)*

7. What does Robinson promise himself during the first storm?

   A. That he will write to his mother more often.

   B. That he will see the world.

   C. That if he survives the storm he will never set sail again.

   D. That he will complain to the captain of the ship.

> Go back and scan Chapter 2 to find the answer.

8. Where does Robinson sail on his second voyage?

   A. Africa

   B. London

   C. York

   D. South America

> Put the voyages that Robinson takes in order.

Type of Question: _____

9. How does Robinson describe most of his voyages?

   A. happy and successful

   B. terrifying and hard

   C. long and dull

   D. unpleasant and full of disappointment

> Find the answer in Chapter 3.

10. How does Robinson make money from his sailing?

   A. He trades and sells goods.

   B. The ship's captain pays him a salary.

   C. He works at the ports where the ships dock.

   D. He is a con man.

> Use the process of elimination to find the answer.

11. What might the remainder of the story be about?

   A. The event that put an end to Robinson's sailing career.

   B. How Robinson returned home to his mother and father.

   C. How Robinson became a ship captain.

   D. None of these seems likely.

> Review the end of Chapter 3 and make a prediction.

Type of Question: _____

Test A   Name: _____

Directions: Read the story called "The Big Snow." Then answer questions 12–22.

The Big Snow

Last year my family and I moved from Miami, Florida to Troy, Vermont. We moved because my mom got a new job at a hospital. My mom is a doctor. She's a heart doctor. She helps people who have diseases in their hearts.

When I found out that we were moving, I was scared. I had lived in Florida my whole life. All of my friends were there. It made me sad to think that I would be leaving them.

One day when I was talking to my dad about it, he said,
    "Hey, Chip, I can think of something good about moving to Vermont."

Think about how the characters feel.

"What's that?" I asked.

"I'll give you a clue. It's cold and white!" my dad replied.

I had forgotten all about snow. It doesn't snow in Florida. The only snow I ever saw was in the movies or on television. Maybe moving wouldn't be so bad after all.

We moved to Vermont in September. My dad told me that it was too early for snow, even in Vermont.

    "Let's keep an eye on the weather forecast," he said. "Before you know it, we will be making a snowman right there in the yard!"

Every day I checked the weather report. Some days it was warm and sunny. Some days there were clouds and rain. There were all kinds of weather. Everything but snow! Vermont was having a warm fall.

One day in November I checked the weather. I couldn't believe what I saw. The forecast said that Troy, Vermont was going to get 10 inches of snow! I measured 10 inches with my ruler. Wow, I thought! That's enough snow to make two snowmen!

What is happening in this part of the story?

The night before the big snow I couldn't sleep. Every half an hour I got up and looked outside to see if I could spot the first flakes falling. After a little while, I fell asleep in front of my bedroom window.

When I got up the next morning the first thing I did was look out of my window. "Wow!" I thought. The whole yard was covered in a thick blanket of snow. The tree branches were covered. The roofs of the houses were covered. Even the seats on my swing set were covered! And the best thing was that the snow was still falling!

| Test A | Name: _____ |

The Big Snow *(cont.)*

I got dressed quickly and ran downstairs. No one else was up yet, so I ran outside. I raced around in circles, making patterns with my footprints. I picked up some snow and tasted it. I even did a somersault. But very soon I was soaked to the bone. I forgot all about the new snow clothes my mom had bought me!

I ran back inside. By then my mom and dad were up. They were pulling on boots and putting on scarves and hats.

"Hey, Chip," my dad said. "You're dressed for Florida snow, not Vermont snow!"

He handed me a pair of new boots, a jacket, a scarf, and gloves. Once I put on all my winter clothes he said, "Now you're ready to rock!"

The three of us ran outside. My mom and dad started to throw snowballs at each other and at me. Then I picked up some snow, packed it in my hand, and threw it back. My first snowball!

"How about that snowman?" I asked Dad.

"Sure, Chip, but we have to follow the correct snowman-making steps."

My dad and I started to make our snowman. Then, my new friend Connie came by with a bunch of raisins and a carrot.

> Pay attention to how the family members act toward each other.

"These are for the eyes and nose," she said.

That night, when I went to bed it was very different than the night before. It seemed that as soon as my head hit the pillow I was sound asleep. The next day and all that week I made snowmen, snow angels, and snowballs. I slid down hills on big pieces of cardboard and made an igloo. I spelled out the letters of my name in snow footprints and rolled around in the snow like a log. At the end of the week of my first big snow I talked to my dad about all the things I did.

"So, Chip, what was your favorite thing about the snow?" Dad asked.

I thought about it for a minute, but I couldn't decide. But I did know one thing. I liked living in Vermont.

Questions 12–22: Select the best answer.

12. Where is Chip from?

A. Troy

B. Vermont

C. Florida

D. Nevada

> Point Right To It!

Type of Question: _____

Test A	Name: _____

The Big Snow *(cont.)*

13. Why did the family move?

   A. They didn't like where they lived.

   B. The mom got a new job.

   C. The dad got a new job.

   D. They always wanted to live where it was snowy.

> Go back and reread the first paragraph.

14. Why do you think Chip feels scared about moving?

   A. He is moving to a rough neighborhood.

   B. He is afraid of flying on an airplane.

   C. New things can often be scary.

   D. He is probably afraid of snow.

> Imagine how you would feel if you had to move to a new place.

Type of Question: _____

15. Why hadn't Chip ever seen real snow before?

   A. He is from a place where it doesn't snow.

   B. He was ill and not allowed out in the cold weather.

   C. He is from the desert.

   D. He is visually impaired.

> Check the fourth paragraph.

16. How does Chip feel about seeing snow for the first time?

   A. scared

   B. bored

   C. disgusted

   D. excited

> Go back and see how the character behaves.

Type of Question: _____

17. What does Chip check every day?

   A. the weather forecast

   B. the air in his bike tires

   C. the forecast in Florida

   D. his back yard

> Go back to the middle of the story to find the answer.

| Test A | Name: _____ |

The Big Snow *(cont.)*

18. Why couldn't Chip sleep?

    A. He was worried about the snow.

    B. He was frightened about the snow.

    C. He was excited about the snow.

    D. He had a virus.

> Read all of the options before you answer.

19. What happened to Chip when he first went out into the snow to play?

    A. He got soaked.

    B. He fell and hurt his arm.

    C. He got lost.

    D. He had a snowball fight with his parents.

> Point Right To It!

Type of Question: _____

20. Why didn't Chip wear the right clothes to play in the snow?

    A. He was too stubborn.

    B. He didn't have the right clothes.

    C. They didn't fit him properly.

    D. He had no idea what to wear in the snow.

> Think about where Chip was from and his experience with snow.

Type of Question: _____

21. Who came over to help him with the snowman?

    A. Chip's mother

    B. Chip's father

    C. Connie

    D. a neighbor

> Point Right To It!

22. How does Chip change from the beginning to the end of the story?

    A. He is scared to move in the beginning but feels good about it at the end.

    B. He dislikes Vermont more than he thought he would.

    C. He misses Florida more than he thought he would.

    D. He feels good about moving to Vermont in the beginning but is scared by the end of the story.

> Go back and reread the end of the story.

Test A   Name: _____

Directions: Read the passage called "How to Make a Snowman." Then answer questions 23–31.

How to Make a Snowman

Making a snowman is not as easy as you think. You have to have just the right kind of snow. It can't be too mushy, and it can't be too dry. Wear gloves if you can. Gloves are better than mittens for snowman building. You have to know how to make very smooth and round balls out of snow. Of course, you have to decide what to use for arms and the face. There are many things to think about to make a snowman just right. If you want to make an excellent snowman, follow these steps below.

What kind of information is in this passage?

Step One: Pack a small amount of snow in your hands to make a smooth, round ball.

Step Two: Roll the small ball in the snow so it gets bigger and bigger. Stop every so often to pack the snow on the ball and smooth it out.

Step Three: Roll the ball until it is about two and a half feet across. This first ball is for the base of the snowman, so it will be the biggest snowball.

Pay attention to the order of the steps.

Step Four: Repeat step two and step three to make two more balls for the middle part of the snowman and the head. The middle ball should be smaller than the bottom ball. The head should be smaller than the middle ball.

Step Five: Place the middle ball on top of the bottom ball.

Step Six: Place the small ball on top of the middle ball.

Step Seven: Pack some snow between each layer so that they stick together.

Step Eight: Make a face for the snowman. For the eyes use raisins, black buttons, or dark jelly beans. Use a carrot for the nose. Use a banana for the mouth.

Step Nine: Put a hat and scarf around the snowman to keep him warm. (It is traditional to use a top hat for a snowman!)

Step Ten: Use sticks for arms.

Voila! You've got your snowman!

Test A   Name: _____

How to Make a Snowman *(cont.)*

Questions 23–31: Select the best answer.

23. What kind of snow is not very good for making a snowman?

   A. mushy

   B. cold

   C. icy

   D. all of these

Type of Question: _____

24. Why might it be better to wear gloves instead of mittens?

   A. Gloves are warmer.

   B. Gloves look better.

   C. Gloves make it easier to form the balls.

   D. Mittens get wet faster.

Type of Question: _____

25. The base of the snowman is made out of which ball?

   A. The second one that you roll.

   B. The third one that you roll.

   C. The first one that you roll.

   D. The fourth one that you roll.

26. How many balls do you make altogether?

   A. 2

   B. 3

   C. 4

   D. 1

Point Right To It!

Think about how you might need to use your fingers.

Review Step Three.

Go back and count the number of balls.

Test A   Name: _____

How to Make a Snowman *(cont.)*

27. What do you do in Step Five?

A. Place the middle ball on top of the bottom ball.

B. Place the bottom ball on top of the middle ball.

C. Place the smallest ball on top of the middle ball.

D. Put a hat on the snowman.

> Review Step Five.

28. What step tells you to pack extra snow between each layer?

A. Step 8

B. Step 9

C. Step 6

D. Step 7

> Review the steps that are listed in the options.

29. Which flavor jelly bean would make the best eyes?

A. cherry

B. vanilla

C. licorice

D. lemon

> Think about the color of the snowman and the color of the jelly beans.

Type of Question: _____

30. Why would a banana make a good mouth?

A. Because it smells good.

B. Because it is curved like a smile.

C. Because birds will eat it.

D. Because it won't melt.

> Think about the shape of the banana.

31. What is the traditional kind of hat a snowman wears?

A. top hat

B. baseball cap

C. cowboy hat

D. straw hat

> Point Right To It!

Type of Question: _____

Test A   Name: _____

Directions: Read the passage called "Amazing Ants." Then answer questions 32–41.

Amazing Ants

No matter where you live you can see ants. Ants can live in most places. They can live in the trunks of old trees and under rocks. Sometimes you can see little mounds of dirt that are the hills that ants live in. There are many different kinds of ants. Ants can be yellow, brown, red, or black. There are millions of ants all over Earth.

What do you expect to learn from this passage?

Ants are insects. That means that ants have many things in common with other types of insects. One thing that all insects have is an exoskeleton. That is kind of like a hard shell. The **exoskeleton** of an ant is like the bones that we have inside of our bodies.

Look at the diagram below to see some of the other parts of the body of an ant. On their heads, ants have two feelers. The feelers are a lot like our noses. The feelers help an ant smell.

The head of the ant also has pinchers. The name of this part tells you something about its job. The pinchers help to carry food, dig, and pinch or fight its enemies.

Because an ant is an insect, it has six legs. You can see that at the end of each leg the ant has a very sharp claw.

Look carefully at the entire diagram before you move forward.

Look carefully at the diagram. What other parts of an insect can you see?

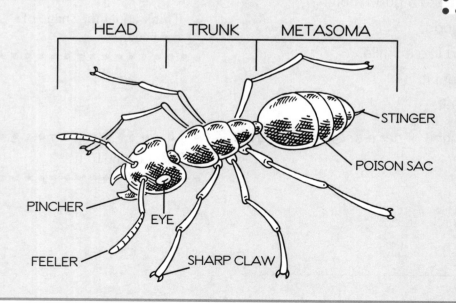

Test A   Name: _____

Amazing Ants *(cont.)*

Ants are **social animals**. That means that they live in groups. Many animals live in groups. Wolves live together in packs, and whales live together in pods. People also live together in groups. The group that ants live in is called a **colony**.

There is much work to do in an ant colony.

1. **The Queen Ant:** The job of the queen ant is to mate and lay eggs. She spends her whole life doing this. The queen has wings.

2. **The Male Ants:** Male ants have wings. The job of the male ants is to mate with the queen so that she can lay eggs. Soon after the male ants mate, they die.

> How is each type of ant different from the others?

3. **The Worker Ant:** Worker ants have the most to do in an ant colony. They are responsible for defending the colony, getting food, and building the nest. Worker ants do not have wings.

Amazing Ant Facts!

- An ant can lift 20 times its own body weight. That means that if you weigh 60 pounds you'd be able to lift something that weighs over 1,000 pounds!

- There are over 12,000 different kinds of ants.

- When ants fight, they usually fight to the death!

- A queen ant can have millions of babies in her single lifetime.

Ants have important jobs to do for our environment. It may not look like it, but they keep things in balance. Ants eat lots of other insects. If they didn't do that, we would have more insects than we could handle on Earth. Ants dig in the soil. When they do that they let air into the earth which keeps it fertilized. Ants also help by spreading the pollen from flowers and the seeds of plants, which help them take root in new places.

> How do you think the author wants the reader to feel about ants?

Ants may be small, but they are survivors that have been on our planet for nearly 100 million years.

Test A | Name: _____

Amazing Ants *(cont.)*

Questions 32–41: Select the best answer.

32. Why do you think the author called this passage "Amazing Ants"?

    A. The author fears ants.

    B. The author respects the work ants do.

    C. The author thinks ants are cute.

    D. The author likes ants.

Type of Question: _____

> Pick the best answer.

33. What colors can ants be?

    A. orange and black

    B. tan and red

    C. yellow and red

    D. all of these

Type of Question: _____

> Point Right To It!

34. What is an exoskeleton?

    A. a kind of hard shell on the outside of the ant's body

    B. the bones on the inside of an ant's body

    C. another name for the feelers on an ant's head

    D. the stinger of the ant

> Go back to paragraph 2 to find the answer.

35. Where is the poison sac on the ant located?

    A. on the back of the ant's body

    B. on the head of the ant

    C. on the tips of the claws

    D. near the eye

> Look carefully at the diagram to find the poison sac.

36. What part of the body does the ant use for smelling?

    A. the pinchers

    B. the feelers

    C. the claws

    D. the exoskeleton

> Go back to paragraph 3 to find the answer.

Test A   Name: _____

Amazing Ants *(cont.)*

37. Social animals are

    A. animals that live together in groups.

    B. animals that live alone.

    C. animals that have exoskeletons.

    D. animals that eat other animals to survive.

> Skim the words that are bold to find the answer.

38. Which type of ant is responsible for defending the colony?

    A. the queen ant

    B. the male ants

    C. the worker ants

    D. the queen, worker, and male ants

> Review the numbered list to find the answer.

Type of Question: _____

39. Why do you think the queen and the male ants have wings?

    A. Wings frighten other animals.

    B. They have to fly into the nest.

    C. It makes them more attractive.

    D. Having wings makes it easier to escape danger.

> Think about how wings help keep animals safe.

40. Why do you think the author has bolded certain words in the passages?

    A. These are important words to learn about ants.

    B. It makes the passage look nicer to have some words bolded.

    C. It makes important words easier to find.

    D. Both A and C.

> Bolded words make information stand out.

Type of Question: _____

41. How do ants help keep the environment healthy?

    A. They eat garbage.

    B. Their digging helps push air into the soil.

    C. They live inside plastic containers.

    D. They live in mounds.

> Reread the end of the passage to find the answer.

Type of Question: _____

Test A Name: _____

Directions: Read the menu for "Jimmy's Big Barbecue Shack." Then answer questions 42–50.

Jimmy's Big Barbecue Shack

Combo Plates   **Available Anytime**

Lunch Plate
2 spare ribs, choice of one side $9.00

Dinner Plate
3 spare ribs, a boneless BBQ chicken breast,
choice of one side. $13.00

Classic BBQ Sampler
3 spare ribs, pulled pork, slaw, baked beans $16.00

Rustling Rib Plate
4 spare ribs, choice of two sides $14.00

Rib Tickler Plate
½ rack of spare ribs with a giant roll. $14.00

> Pay attention to how the menu is organized.

Sandwiches / Add fountain drink for $1.50

Pulled Pork BBQ
Hickory-smoked pork pulled and served on a soft roll with
Jimmy's special original BBQ sauce. $6.00

Famous Texas BBQ Beef
Slow-smoked beef brisket sliced thin and served on a soft
roll with Jimmy's special original BBQ sauce $7.00

BBQ Chicken Breast
Juicy chicken breast cooked on the grill and smothered
in Jimmy's special original BBQ sauce. $7.00

Italian Sausage
Sweet Italian sausage done on the grill with peppers and
onions and served with Jimmy's secret mustard sauce $7.00

> How is this section different from the one above?

Grilled Portobello
Onion, tomato, and a slice of mozzarella on a soft roll
(vegetarian friendly) $8.00

Beef Brisket Reuben
Sliced brisket, slaw, Swiss cheese on rye bread with
Jimmy's homemade Russian dressing $8.00

Test A   Name: _____

Jimmy's Big Barbecue Shack *(cont.)*

Sides   All sides are made fresh daily

	Reg. (8 oz.)	Pt. (16 oz.)	Qt. (32 oz.)
BBQ Baked Beans	$3.25	$6.00	$10.00
Georgia Slaw	$2.75	$5.00	$10.00
Cajun Corn Salad	$3.25	$5.50	$10.00
Spicy Collard Greens	$3.25	$5.50	$10.00
Grandma's Tater Salad	$2.75	$5.00	$9.00
10 Spice Fries	$3.00	$4.50	$7.00

> What can you find on this part of the menu?

Desserts   All desserts are made fresh daily

Baked Apple Pie with Vanilla Ice Cream $5.50

Peach Crumble with a Dollop of Cream. $6.00

Pecan Pie $7.00

Grandma's Famous Red Velvet Cake $7.50

Drinks

Iced Tea or Coffee $2.50

Bottle or Fountain Soda. $2.00

Assorted Juices $2.25

Lemonade $3.00

To Place an Order

Order online at *www.jimmysbbqshack.com*

Phone Orders at 1-800-555-4321

Let Jimmy's Big Barbecue Shack cater your next event!

> What kind of information can you find here?

- Birthdays
- Graduations
- Weddings
- Family Reunions
- School Picnics

Test A   Name: _____

Jimmy's Big Barbecue Shack *(cont.)*

Questions 42–50: Select the best answer.

42. Who most likely owns this restaurant?

    A. Grandma

    B. It is impossible to say.

    C. someone named Jimmy

    D. someone whose last name is Shack

> Look for clues that may tell you this information.

Type of Question: _____

43. How many Combo Plates can you select from?

    A. 5

    B. 6

    C. 11

    D. 17

> Find the Combo Plate section and count how many.

44. How many ribs do you get with the Classic BBQ Sampler?

    A. 2

    B. 4

    C. 12

    D. 3

> Look for this menu item and read the description.

45. If you order a pulled-pork sandwich with a fountain drink, how much can you expect to pay?

    A. $7.50

    B. $6.00

    C. $1.50

    D. $8.50

> Reread the Sandwich section of the menu.

46. What is the likely reason Jimmy calls one of his menu items Famous Texas BBQ Beef?

    A. He thinks it is the best thing on the menu.

    B. It is not served anywhere else in the country.

    C. It is the most popular menu item.

    D. It is only $7.00.

> Think about what *famous* means.

Type of Question: _____

Test A Name: _____

Jimmy's Big Barbecue Shack *(cont.)*

47. Which item on the menu does not have any meat?

   A. Beef Brisket Reuben

   B. Grilled Portobello

   C. Lunch Plate

   D. Italian Sausage

> Look for clues on the menu.

48. If you order the Lunch Plate, which of the following could you order with it?

   A. collard greens

   B. baked potato

   C. mac and cheese

   D. onion rings

Type of Question: _____

> Review the sides that are available.

49. What does Qt. mean?

   A. quarter

   B. pint

   C. quarter-pounder

   D. quart

> Use information in the same area to help you answer.

50. What does it mean if something is made daily?

   A. When they run out they make more.

   B. It is made every day.

   C. It is made once a week.

   D. It is made when someone orders it.

> Eliminate options that are silly or don't seem to make much sense.

Test B   Name: _____

Directions: Read the passage entitled "Teeth." Then answer questions 1–11.

Teeth

> Scan the test questions before you begin to read.

Baby Teeth

When you are born you have a brain, a heart, and two lungs. You are born with most of the organs you will need to live a healthy life. But there is something very important that you are not born with. It takes many years for you to grow these things that you will need to survive. Can you imagine what they are? They are your teeth!

You have probably seen a newborn baby. Newborn babies don't have any teeth at all. This is why they can only drink milk and why they eat very soft foods. They would not be able to chew anything else. But babies don't stay toothless for long. When they get to be about 6 months old, their first teeth start to poke through their gums. This is called *teething*, and it can be painful. Babies cry a lot when they begin to get their first teeth.

By the time babies are 3, they usually have their first set of teeth. This first set of teeth is called **primary teeth**. There are 20 primary teeth in all. But they don't stick around for very long. When a person gets a little bit older, about 5 or 6, these primary teeth begin to fall out one at a time. They are replaced by a set of **permanent teeth**. The permanent teeth are the teeth you have for the rest of your life.

By the time you are about 13 years old, you have most of your permanent teeth. There are 28 permanent teeth in all. At about 18 years old, you get four more teeth. They are called wisdom teeth. They grow in the very back of your mouth. Sometimes wisdom teeth can hurt. Many people have to have them removed. Some people never get them at all.

> Scan the headings and sub-headings before you read.

The Tooth Fairy

In many places in the world, something special happens when you lose a baby tooth. You put the tooth under your pillow. Then you go to sleep. During the night the Tooth Fairy comes. She takes your lost tooth away. In its place she leaves a small sum of money. It's not so bad losing a tooth if you know you will trade it for money!

Parts of the Tooth

The part of the tooth that you can see is only "the tip of the iceberg!" That means that there is much more to the tooth below the gum, where you can't see it. Look at the diagram on the next page to study all of the parts of the tooth.

Test B   Name: _____

Teeth (cont.)

Tooth Anatomy

Crown

— Enamel
— Dentin
— Pulp
— Gums
— Cementum

Root

What kind of information does this diagram provide?

Types of Teeth

If you take a good look inside of your mouth, you will see that your teeth are different sizes. This has to do with the type of work they do.

Your two front teeth and the two teeth on either side of them are called incisors. You have eight incisors altogether. You have four on the top and four on the bottom. *Incisors* are the teeth that cut and chop into food. If you can picture eating an ear of corn then you can see what type of work incisors do!

Next to your incisors you have two very pointy teeth like fangs. These are called canines. You have two on the top and two on the bottom. You can see canine teeth in cats and dogs, only they are much longer and sharper! *Canine teeth* help to tear food, like meat, apart.

Next to your canines you have teeth called premolars. Premolars are flat. They have ridges on them. You have four premolars on the top and four on the bottom. The rest of your teeth are called molars. You have four on the top and four on the bottom. *Premolars* and *molars* are good at grinding and mashing food. This makes the food smaller so it is easier to swallow.

Imagine eating an apple. It is easy to see how the different types of teeth work. You bite into the apple with your incisors. The incisors cut pieces of the apple away. The canines help to shred the apple into smaller bits. The premolars and molars chomp up and down, mashing the apple into even tinier bits.

Test B | Name: _____

Teeth *(cont.)*

Caring for Your Teeth

Your permanent teeth have to last your entire lifetime. It is important to keep them healthy. To take care of your teeth, do these things:

1. Brush your teeth twice a day. Make sure to brush the back and front of your teeth.

2. Use dental floss to clean the spaces between your teeth. A toothbrush can't reach everywhere.

3. Go to the dentist twice a year for a check-up. Even if you need to have a cavity filled, it is better than losing a tooth!

Without teeth, you would not be able to talk the way you do. Without teeth, you would not be able to eat the things that you like to eat. And a smile looks great with a nice set of chompers!

Glossary

cementum: covers the root of the tooth

crown: the white part of the tooth that you can see

dentin: tough material that covers the pulp

enamel: a hard, shiny material that covers the crown

gum: soft, pink part around your tooth

jawbone: the bone that your tooth is anchored in

pulp: inner part of the tooth where the nerves are located

> How does this glossary connect to the diagram?

Questions 1–11: Select the best answer.

1. When do babies first start to get teeth?

    A. around 6 months old

    B. around 3 years old

    C. around 13 years old

    D. immediately

> Reread the section called Baby Teeth.

Test B   Name: _____

Teeth *(cont.)*

2. What is your first set of teeth called?

   A. permanent teeth

   B. firsties

   C. primary teeth

   D. premolars

Type of Question: _____

> Key words are bolded.

3. How many teeth are there in a baby's first set?

   A. 28

   B. 8

   C. 25

   D. 20

> Scan the Baby Teeth section and look for numerals.

4. About how old are you when you have most of your permanent teeth?

   A. 3 years old

   B. 17 years old

   C. 13 years old

   D. 19 years old

> Scan the passage to find the bolded words.

5. How did wisdom teeth likely get their name?

   A. They were named by a dentist called Dr. Wisdom.

   B. You get them when you are older and probably smarter.

   C. The sooner your wisdom teeth come in the smarter you become.

   D. It is wise to have them removed.

> Use what you know plus story clues to answer.

Type of Question: _____

| Test B | Name: _____ |

Teeth *(cont.)*

6. How many different types of teeth do you have?

    A. 4

    B. 28

    C. 20

    D. 32

> Find the section that talks about types of teeth.

7. Where are the nerves in the tooth located?

    A. in the crown

    B. in the cementum

    C. in the jawbone

    D. in the pulp

> Look at the diagram and glossary.

8. Where are your premolars located?

    A. next to the incisors

    B. behind the molars

    C. next to your canines

    D. behind the wisdom teeth

> Scan the passage for the word *premolars*.

Type of Question: _____

9. Your canines would be very useful if you were eating

    A. a slice of pizza.

    B. a steak.

    C. corn on the cob.

    D. ice cream.

> Think about what the canines do to the food.

Type of Question: _____

Test B   Name: _____

Teeth *(cont.)*

10. Which teeth would you use the most if you ate nothing but fruits and vegetables?

    A. molars

    B. incisors

    C. canines

    D. wisdom teeth

Type of Question: _____

> Think about the job of each type of tooth.

11. How are the words in the glossary arranged?

    A. by order of importance

    B. alphabetical order

    C. by which is the most sensitive

    D. There is no order.

> Think about other glossaries you have used.

Test B   Name: _____

Directions: Read the poem entitled "The Owl and the Pussycat." Then answer questions 12–21.

The Owl and the Pussycat
by
Edward Lear

> Who is this poem about?

I The Owl and the Pussy-cat went to sea
In a beautiful pea-green boat,
They took some honey, and plenty of money,
Wrapped up in a five-pound note.
The Owl looked up to the stars above,
And sang to a small guitar,
"O lovely Pussy! O Pussy, my love,
What a beautiful Pussy you are,
You are,
You are!
What a beautiful Pussy you are!"

II Pussy said to the Owl, "You elegant fowl!
How charmingly sweet you sing!
O let us be married! Too long we have tarried:
But what shall we do for a ring?"
They sailed away, for a year and a day,
To the land where the Bong-Tree grows
And there in a wood a Piggy-wig stood
With a ring at the end of his nose,
His nose,
His nose,
With a ring at the end of his nose.

> What do the characters want to do?

III "Dear Pig, are you willing to sell for one shilling
Your ring?" Said the Piggy, "I will."
So they took it away, and were married next day
By the Turkey who lives on the hill.
They dined on mince, and slices of quince,
Which they ate with a runcible spoon;
And hand in hand, on the edge of the sand,
They danced by the light of the moon,
The moon,
The moon,
They danced by the light of the moon.

Test B   Name: _____

The Owl and the Pussycat *(cont.)*

Questions 12–21: Select the best answer.

12. What color is the boat that the owl and the pussycat sail away in?

    A. honey

    B. green

    C. pink

    D. red

> Go back to stanza 1 to find the answer.

13. Which animal plays the guitar?

    A. the pig

    B. the pussycat

    C. the owl

    D. the turkey

> Read each option before you answer.

Type of Question: _____

14. Which of the following best describes the poem?

    A. realistic

    B. science fiction

    C. fantasy

    D. fable

> Use the process of elimination.

15. What do the owl and the pussycat want to do?

    A. have a party

    B. go sailing

    C. get married

    D. sing songs

> Reread stanza 2 to find the answer.

16. What do the owl and the pussycat take with them?

    A. clean clothes

    B. fancy clothes

    C. peas

    D. honey and money

> Go back to the beginning of the poem to see what they packed.

| Test B | Name: _____ |

The Owl and the Pussycat *(cont.)*

17. Which word or words in the second stanza is a homophone?

    A. ring

    B. fowl

    C. stood

    D. Both A and B.

> Homophones sound alike, but have different meanings.

18. Where do the owl and the pussycat get a ring?

    A. from the turkey

    B. they bring it with them

    C. from the pig

    D. under the Bong-Tree

> Recall the different animals they meet.

Type of Question: _____

19. What is a shilling?

    A. money

    B. a guitar

    C. a moon

    D. a spoon

> Look for a context clue to help determine the meaning.

20. Where are the owl and the pussycat dancing?

    A. on a beach

    B. on their boat

    C. on a hill

    D. It is impossible to say.

> Make an inference by using clues from the poem.

Type of Question: _____

21. Why are the owl and the pussycat an unlikely couple?

    A. Owls like turkeys.

    B. Cats like pigs.

    C. Cats and birds usually don't get along.

    D. Cats like to dance, and owls don't.

> What do you know about cats and birds?

Type of Question: _____

Test B	Name: _____

Directions: Read the passage entitled "America's National Monuments." Then answer questions 22–30.

America's National Monuments

The Statue of Liberty is a famous place in our country. It is in New York Harbor. It is a special place for Americans. The Statue of Liberty is called a national monument. A national monument can be a place or a building. Monuments honor important people. They show respect for events and ideas. The Statue of Liberty stands for freedom and hope. There are 101 national monuments in the United States. They are all over the country. Maybe there is one in your state or even in your city.

1. Booker T. Washington National Monument

Where: **Virginia**
Made a monument: **April, 1956**

> How is the information organized?

Booker T. Washington was born into slavery in 1856. He was an important leader in the African-American community. He was a teacher. He was a writer. He spoke out against slavery. There are many schools named after him. The monument in his name is part of the plantation where he was born as a slave. If you visit the Booker T. Washington Monument, you will see a house that looks just like the one that Booker grew up in.

2. California Coastal

Where: **California**
Made a monument: **January, 2011**

California Coastal is not a place that has been made by people. It is not a house. It is not a statue. It is a natural place. It is the 840-mile rocky coastline of the state of California. Along this coast there are reefs and rocks. Many animals live in these places. Because it is a national monument, it is protected. It will be kept clean and safe. The animals will not be hurt. It also means that in the future, Americans will be able to visit this place and see its beauty.

3. Devil's Tower

Where: **Wyoming**
Made a monument: **September, 1906**

> What information does each entry have?

Devil's Tower is our first national monument. It is a huge rock formation that is over 1,000 feet high. It rises straight up out of the ground. It looks like a giant tube made of rock. It is so big that it can be seen for miles and miles. Devil's Tower was very important to many Native American tribes. They thought of it as a holy place. Today, Devil's Tower is a place that hikers and rock climbers like to climb.

Test B	Name: _____

America's National Monuments *(cont.)*

4. Fort McHenry

Where: Maryland
Made a monument: March, 1925

Fort McHenry is an army fort that is shaped like a star. It is in the Baltimore Harbor. In 1812, the United States was at war with Britain. It was called the War of 1812. The powerful British ships bombed Fort McHenry from the Chesapeake Bay for hours and hours. The soldiers inside of the fort hit the ships back with cannon fire. They were able to defend the fort and stop the British. The "Star-Spangled Banner" was written about this famous battle.

> Think how these places or people are important to our history.

5. George Washington Birthplace

Where: Virginia
Made a monument: January, 1930

George Washington was the first president of the United States. He is called the Father of Our Country. Before he was the president, he was a general. He fought in the Revolutionary War. He helped us to win our freedom from the British. If you visit this monument you will see the house where George Washington was born in 1732. It is the house he grew up in. Some parts of the house look just like they did when he was a boy.

6. Navajo

Where: Arizona
Made a monument: March, 1909

The Anasazi were Native Americans who lived in Arizona. They lived there hundreds of years before white people from Europe came. They built homes high up in the cliffs of the desert. These homes are called cliff dwellings. If you visit this national monument, you will see the ancient homes of these early Americans.

There are only six monuments listed here, but there are so many others. There are monuments in Alaska, Hawaii, and Maine. Some monuments are under water. Others are right in the middle of big cities. Some monuments were made by people. Others were made by nature.

All monuments tell a story. America's monuments tell us about our past. They show what and who we think is important. They tell what we believe is worth protecting. America's monuments tell us about us. They stand for who we are.

Test B   Name: _____

America's National Monuments *(cont.)*

Questions 22–30: Select the best answer.

22. What is a national monument?

    A. a special place for Americans to visit

    B. The Statue of Liberty

    C. a place or building that honors a person, an event, or an idea

    D. a place that stands for freedom and hope

> Reread the first paragraph.

23. How many national monuments are there?

    A. 50

    B. 101

    C. 10

    D. 161

> Point Right To It!

Type of Question: _____

24. Why did the author put Devil's Tower after California Coastal?

    A. She likes California Coastal more than Devil's Tower.

    B. California Coastal is more important than Devil's Tower.

    C. More people visit California Coastal than Devil's Tower.

    D. D comes after C in the alphabet.

> Look for a pattern in how the text is organized.

25. What does the date on each entry mean?

    A. It is the date each place was made a monument.

    B. It is the date that each monument was discovered.

    C. It is the date that each monument was built.

    D. none of these

> Look back at the text next to each date.

Test B   Name: _____

America's National Monuments *(cont.)*

26. Which of the following monuments is *not* man-made?

   A. Fort McHenry

   B. Booker T. Washington National Monument

   C. Navajo

   D. Devil's Tower

> Think of what the opposite of "man-made" is.

27. Where is Fort McHenry?

   A. Maryland

   B. Virginia

   C. Britain

   D. New York Harbor

> Go back and scan that entry.

Type of Question: _____

28. What would you find at the Navajo monument?

   A. holy places of Native Americans

   B. the site of a famous battle

   C. cliff dwellings of the Anasazi

   D. ancient drawings on the rocks in the desert

> Read each option carefully.

29. Which of the following is most likely a national monument?

   A. Disney World

   B. the house in America that President Obama grew up in

   C. the first car made in America

   D. the home where George Washington Carver was born

> Make a deduction.

Type of Question: _____

30. What does the author mean by "They stand for who we are"?

   A. Monuments tell what we value and think is important.

   B. Monuments are interesting places to visit.

   C. Having monuments means we are a country.

   D. Some events and people are more important than others.

> Reread the last paragraph.

Test B   Name: _____

Directions: Read the story called "Three Swinging Pigs and a Wolf." Then answer questions 31–40.

Three Swinging Pigs and a Wolf

Once upon a time there lived three little pigs. They were called Pink, Dink, and Stink. Pink got his name because he was the pinkest pig that anyone had ever seen. He was the color of cotton candy. Dink was short for Dinky. Dink got his name because he was very small for his age. He was the runt of the litter. The runt is the smallest animal born. And Stink, well, you can pretty much guess how he got his name.

··· What kind of story is this? ···

Pink, Dink, and Stink lived in a little cottage in the woods. They loved where they lived. They had so many good friends and neighbors. Right next door to them lived Mrs. Betty Badger. She was the one in the town that made sure that everyone followed the rules. As long as you behaved yourself, Betty was your best friend. But if you broke a rule, like playing your music too loud, well, then she would bug you about it until you turned it down!

In the house on the other side of the pigs lived Mr. Ralph Raccoon. He slept most of the day because he had a night job as a mechanic. There was no kind of car or truck that Ralph couldn't fix. Ralph was so good at fixing things that if anyone ever had a broken pipe or a stuck window, they would call Ralph. Ralph would have it working in no time at all.

Now, in their backyard, the pigs had a shiny, new swing set. This swing set was their pride and joy. It was white with red stripes, so it looked very much like a candy cane.

On each end of the swing set there was a giant slide. The slides curved around like locks of hair. At the bottom of each slide there was a huge puddle of mud. In between the slides there were three swings. Each swing had the name of a little pig painted on the seat.

Every morning after breakfast, the little pigs ran out of their house to play on their candy-cane swing set. They raced up the ladder steps of the slides and hollered "Weeeeee!" as they slid down and splashed into a mud puddle. Then they would rush over and hop onto their swings.

"Push me, push me," Stink would say to Pink.

··· What is happening here? ···

"No! You push me!" Stink would reply.

The little pigs had a problem. The problem was their tiny, little legs. If you know anything about getting high up on a swing, it's that you have to use your legs to push and pull. But no matter how hard the little pigs pumped their legs back and forth, they just couldn't get very high.

Test B   Name: _____

Three Swinging Pigs and a Wolf *(cont.)*

They always needed a push, which meant that they could never swing, all three of them, at the same time.

First, Stink would take a turn pushing Pink and Dink. Then Dink would push Stink and Pink. It was exhausting!

"We have to figure out a way for us to all swing at the same time," Dink said.

"I have an idea," Pink chimed in. "Let's get Betty Badger to come and push us."

Betty did her best, but it didn't work so well. She had to scurry back and forth between the swings to give each piggy a push and, after a few times, she got tired out.

"I've got better things to do with my time," Betty cried out, "than push a bunch of piggies on their swings! And besides, you fellows better keep all of the wee-weeing down!"

Next, they called upon the talents of Ralph Raccoon.

> How do the pigs try to solve their problem?

"Can you build us some kind of gadget that will do the pushing for us?" Stink asked.

"Interesting," said Ralph, "I have an idea."

Ralph installed a crank on one end of the swing set. The crank was attached by a pulley which was fixed to a stationary bike. Ralph got on the bike. The three pigs got on their swings. Ralph began to pedal on the bike, which turned the crank, which pushed the swings back and forth.

"Weeeee," cried Pink.

"Weeeee," cried Stink.

"Weeeee," cried Dink.

"Ouch," cried Ralph.

Ralph fell off of the bike.

"My knee! I hurt my knee."

"Oh, well," Pink said sadly. "I guess we will never all be able to swing at the same time."

A few days later, when Pink, Stink, and Dink were rolling in their giant mud puddle, along came the big bad wolf. He stopped in front of their house and stared at them as they played in the mud.

"I have an idea," Pink said to his brothers. "Why don't we get the big bad wolf to huff and puff and blow us on our swings?"

Dink and Stink thought for a minute. They knew that the wolf certainly had a powerful enough huffer and puffer to blow them back and forth, but he was such a mean thing, and only used his talents to knock houses down. They didn't think that he would be willing to help.

Test B   Name: _____

Three Swinging Pigs and a Wolf *(cont.)*

"It's true that he's mean," said Pink. "But he's also lonely. He doesn't have any friends because of his bad reputation. Perhaps I can convince him that helping us would make him more likeable. Just go along with me, and we'll see what happens."

The wolf continued to stare at the pigs with his eyes narrowed into slits.

"What do you want?" Pink shouted at the wolf.

"You know exactly what I want. Why, I want to…"

"We know. We know," said Dink. "You want to huff, and you want to puff, and you want to blow our house down. It's so boring. Don't you ever want to do anything else? Something different?"

"What do you mean? I am a big bad wolf. Big bad wolves huff, and puff, and blow houses down. It's what we do. It's a tradition."

"So what?" said Stink. "You have to do what every other wolf does? You can't think for yourself?"

> Think about what the pig says.

"Of course I can think for myself."

"You know this is why you don't have any friends. Cause you're such a meanie."

"I know. I know," said the wolf. "But what can I do? Huffing and puffing only destroys. It knocks things over. It smashes things to bits."

"It doesn't have to be that way," Dink said. "We have an idea."

So the three pigs explained all about the swing problem to the big bad wolf. They told him how sad they were that they could not, all three of them, swing together. They explained how Betty Badger and Ralph Raccoon had tried to help but couldn't.

"Well, what can I do?" asked the wolf.

"Come with us," said the pigs, "and we will show you."

So the wolf went into the backyard. The three pigs hopped onto their swings.

"Now," squealed Pink, "stand behind us and do what you do best."

Suddenly, the wolf understood exactly what the pigs wanted him to do. So he huffed, and he puffed, and he blew with all of his might on the little backs of the little pigs on their little swings. Finally, the little pigs swung high up into the air and then back again. They swung all together back and forth and back and forth. They were so happy that all three shouted, *"Weeeeee!"* so loudly that Mrs. Badger came running out of her house in her slippers, and Ralph Raccoon woke up in the middle of the day!

Test B   Name: _____

Three Swinging Pigs and a Wolf *(cont.)*

The big bad wolf blew the swinging piggies all afternoon until his huffer and his puffer needed a rest. For the first time in his life, the wolf used his natural talents to help, and not hurt. He now had three friends, and he was very happy. And for the first time since they had their swing set the pigs were able to swing together, so they were happy too.

The three little piggies and the big bad wolf became friends, such good friends that if you happen to walk past their house in the late afternoon, you might even see the big bad wolf rolling around in a giant puddle of mud!

Questions 31–40: Select the best answer.

31. What type of story is this?

    A. fable

    B. fairy tale

    C. fiction

    D. nonfiction

> Think of other stories that begin and end the same way.

32. What is the relationship between the pigs?

    A. They are friends.

    B. They are brothers.

    C. They are neighbors.

    D. They are sisters.

> Look for story clues.

33. If there was a fourth pig, which of the following would most likely be his name?

    A. Jeb

    B. Lucky

    C. Link

    D. Curley

> Use the process of elimination.

Type of Question: _____

Test B   Name: _____

Three Swinging Pigs and a Wolf *(cont.)*

34. What is the problem in the story?

   A. The wolf is going to blow down the pigs' house.

   B. Mrs. Badger won't let the pigs play on their swings.

   C. Mr. Raccoon can't fix the swings.

   D. The pigs can't swing all at the same time.

> Go back and check the story.

35. How would you best describe Betty Badger?

   A. sweet

   B. lazy

   C. mean

   D. bossy

> Think about the character's behavior.

Type of Question: _____

36. How does Mr. Raccoon's gadget work?

   A. It uses a giant fan to blow the pigs back and forth on their swings.

   B. It uses a bike to pull a pulley that turns a crank.

   C. It lifts the swings up with levers and then drops them down very quickly.

   D. Mr. Raccoon runs back and forth and pushes the pigs with a giant broom.

37. How do the pigs convince the wolf to help them?

   A. They offer to pay him.

   B. They threaten to call Mrs. Badger.

   C. They say they will let him blow part of their house down.

   D. They explain that if he wasn't so mean he might have some friends.

> Review what the pigs say to the wolf.

| Test B | Name: _____ |

Three Swinging Pigs and a Wolf *(cont.)*

38. What do the pigs say the wolf can't do?

    A. be nice

    B. think for himself

    C. blow their house down

    D. make friends

> Point Right To It!

39. How is the wolf able to help the pigs swing together?

    A. He blows on their backs, and this pushes the pigs back and forth.

    B. He uses his four powerful legs.

    C. He builds a machine called the Pigswinger.

    D. He gets some of his wolf friends to help.

> Look for the solution to the problem.

40. What is the main theme of the story?

    A. the importance of friendship

    B. the importance of bravery

    C. the importance of solving problems together

    D. the importance of using your talents to help and not hurt

> Pick the one that makes the most sense to you.

Type of Question: _____

Test B   Name: _____

Directions: Read the passage entitled "All About Pasta." Then answer questions 41–50.

> Scan the passage before you begin to read.

All About Pasta

Pasta is a food that many people like to eat. Think about it just for a moment. When was the last time you ate some pasta? Maybe it was only yesterday!

Pasta comes from Italy. It is made from wheat and flour. Pasta is a healthy food. Pasta is called a staple food. A staple food is a food that you can eat almost every day.

Pasta comes in lots of different shapes and sizes. This is one of the things that makes it so much fun to cook and eat! The next time you are at the store, count how many types of pasta you see.

Most pasta is made with a simple recipe. You mix two different kinds of flour, eggs, water, and a pinch of salt together. Then you knead the pasta with your hands until it is a soft, smooth ball. Next, you roll it out with a rolling pin. Last, you feed the flat dough into a pasta machine. You can set the machine so that it will cut the pasta into whatever shape and size you want.

> What is this section about?

There are over 100 different types of pasta. Some are long and thin. Others are shaped like elbows or wheels. And there are many types of pasta that are shaped like little tubes.

 Capellini: This pasta is long and thin. "Capellini" means *little hairs* in Italian.

 Farfalle: This pasta is shaped like a butterfly. "Farfalle" means *butterfly* in Italian.

 Gomito: This pasta looks like little bent tubes. You may also know these as macaroni. "Gomito" means *elbow* in Italian.

 Lumaconi: This large pasta is shaped like the shell of a big snail. "Lumaconi" means *large snails* in Italian.

 Penne: This pasta looks like a medium-sized tube with the ends cut on a slant. "Penne" means *pens* in Italian.

Test B Name: _____

All About Pasta *(cont.)*

 Rigatoni: This pasta looks like short, fat tubes with ridges on them. "Rigatoni" means *large lined ones* in Italian.

 Rotelle: This pasta is shaped like a wagon wheel. "Rotelle" means *little wheels* in Italian.

 Spaghetti: This pasta looks like long rods. "Spaghetti" means *little twines* in Italian.

How to Cook Pasta

How to cook pasta depends on its shape and size. The smaller the pasta is, the less time it has to be cooked. The larger the pasta is, the more time it will need to be cooked. Here are the basic steps for cooking pasta:

1. Fill a large pot with water.
2. When the water boils, add about 1 tablespoon of salt.
3. Wait a moment until the water is really boiling.
4. Add the pasta.
5. Stir it around with a spoon so it does not stick to the pot.
6. Check the box to see how long to cook the pasta.
7. When it is almost done, fish out one piece.
8. Blow on it to cool it off.
9. Test it. It should be soft on the outside and a little bit hard on the inside.
10. If the pasta is finished, drain it with a colander.

> What can you learn from this section?

How to Serve Pasta

Pasta can be served in lots of ways. Some people like pasta with olive oil and some fresh cheese. Other folks like a thick red sauce spread over their pasta. Pasta can be served with meat or with grilled vegetables.

Do you Twist or Cut?

There are two ways you can eat long noodles. You can twist them or cut them. Look at the diagrams below to see which one matches the way you eat pasta.

| Test B | Name: _____ |

All About Pasta *(cont.)*

Questions 41–50: Select the best answer.

41. What country does pasta come from?

    A. United States

    B. Italy

    C. Europe

    D. China

> Point Right To It!

Type of Question: _____

42. What is a staple food?

    A. a dessert

    B. a food you can eat on special holidays, like Thanksgiving

    C. a healthy food

    D. a food that you can eat almost every day

> Point Right To It!

43. Which of the following is most likely a staple food?

    A. bread

    B. ice cream

    C. broccoli

    D. water

> Make a deduction.

Type of Question: _____

44. Which of the following is not a step in making pasta?

    A. adding the salt

    B. kneading the dough

    C. adding the eggs

    D. adding the milk

> Reread the paragraph where making pasta is explained.

45. Which pasta is the most like capellini?

    A. spaghetti

    B. penne

    C. farfalle

    D. rotelle

> Compare the shapes of the pasta.

| Test B | Name: _____ |

All About Pasta *(cont.)*

46. Which pasta looks like an elbow?

 A. rigatoni

 B. farfalle

 C. gomito

 D. lumaconi

Reread the descriptions of the pasta shapes.

47. Which pasta probably takes the longest to cook?

 A. lumaconi

 B. gomito

 C. penne

 D. rotelle

Use clues from the passage to make a deduction.

Type of Question: _____

48. What do you add to the boiling water in which you cook the pasta?

 A. sugar

 B. salt

 C. pepper

 D. cheese

Pick the one that makes the most sense.

49. Which pasta would be the best for twirling?

 A. farfelle

 B. penne

 C. capellini

 D. rotelle

Picture the shapes of each pasta.

50. How do you know if the pasta is cooked?

 A. It will be mushy.

 B. It will be cooled off.

 C. It will be crunchy.

 D. It will be soft on the outside and a little bit hard on the inside.

Reread the section on cooking pasta.

Test C   Name: _____

Directions: Read the passage called "The First Aid Kit." Then answer questions 1–10.

The First Aid Kit

Have you ever seen a first aid kit? A first aid kit is full of things that you can use in an emergency. An emergency is when a person gets hurt and they are not near a hospital or a doctor. You can use the things in a first aid kit until help arrives.

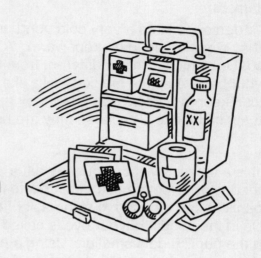

It is important to know what a first aid kit looks like. A first aid kit can be a large metal box, or it can be made of cloth. A first aid kit usually has a red or white cross on the outside of it. It will also say **First Aid Kit**.

Gloves

A first aid kit will have gloves. The gloves are made from a special material. They are very thin. You throw them away after you use them. Gloves help to protect the person who has been hurt. They also protect the person who is helping. There can be germs on your hands. If a person has a cut, you don't want the germs from your hands to enter the wound. Also, if a person is bleeding, you want to make sure that the blood doesn't touch your hands.

Bandages

A first aid kit will have different kinds of bandages. Bandages are used to cover cuts or scrapes. Some bandages are as simple as Band-Aids®. These are the kind where you peel the back away and then stick it on the skin to cover the wound. There are other bandages called butterfly strips. These are used when a person has a deeper cut that may need stitches. They work like a Band-Aid except they pull the skin together to try to help close the wound.

Soap, Wipes, and Cotton Balls

A first aid kit will have some things you can use to clean a cut or scrape. There may be bar soap. There may also be wipes that are inside of a little package. These wipes have a strong smell. That is because they are soaked in a liquid called *antiseptic*. This helps to kill any germs that may be on the cut. The kit will also have cotton to dab onto the wound to clean up any dirt or blood that may be on it. The wound must be cleaned before it can be covered.

Test C	Name: _____

The First Aid Kit *(cont.)*

Space Blanket

Let's say a person fell into a very cold pond or lake. After they were rescued they would need to be kept warm. A first aid kit has something called a space blanket. This is different from the kind of blanket that you have on your bed. A space blanket looks like it is made from foil. These blankets can keep a person warm, but they are very lightweight. They are called space blankets because they are used by astronauts.

Penlight

A penlight is a tiny flashlight. You may have seen one the last time you went to the doctor. Doctors use penlights to look up your nose or in your ears. A penlight can be used to shine a light into a person's eye. The black circle in the middle of your eye is called the pupil. When a light is shined on the pupil, it gets smaller. Using a penlight can help show how badly a person is hurt. If you shine the penlight on a person's eye and the pupil doesn't change, it can mean they have a serious injury.

Thermometer

A thermometer measures how hot or cold someone is. The normal body temperature is 98.6 degrees. It can be dangerous if your temperature rises too much higher than 98.6. This is why it is important to take a person's temperature when they get hurt. If you know that someone has a fever and is too hot, then you can put ice packs on them. If you know that someone is too cold, then you can wrap them in a space blanket.

These are just a few of the things that are in a first aid kit. Some first aid kits have much more. You should learn how to use everything in a first aid kit. You never know when you may need to help. If you don't know how to use the things in the kit, you might wind up hurting someone without meaning to.

Questions 1–10: Select the best answer.

1. Where might you use a first aid kit?

    A. in the hospital

    B. at the doctor's office

    C. at the mall

    D. none of these

Test C | Name: _____

The First Aid Kit *(cont.)*

2. How can you tell if something is a first aid kit?

A. It will have a cross on the outside.

B. It will have a cross on the inside.

C. It will be a metal box.

D. It will be made of cloth.

3. What do you do with the gloves in a first aid kit after you use them?

A. Fold them up and put them back into the first aid kit.

B. Turn them inside out and put them back into the first aid kit.

C. Give them to the person you have helped.

D. Throw them away.

4. How is a butterfly strip different from a Band-Aid?

A. It is bigger.

B. It pulls the skin together.

C. It pulls the skin apart.

D. It is only used for burns.

5. What is an antiseptic?

A. a type of glove

B. something used on burns only

C. a liquid that kills germs

D. a bar of soap

6. What color would a space blanket most likely be?

A. red

B. silver

C. purple

D. pink

Test C   Name: _____

The First Aid Kit *(cont.)*

7. How did the space blanket get its name?

    A. It is used by astronauts.

    B. It doesn't take up that much space.

    C. It is lightweight.

    D. It was invented by a woman whose last name is Space.

8. What happens when you shine the penlight into the eye of a healthy person?

    A. The pupil gets larger.

    B. The eye closes.

    C. The eye opens.

    D. The pupil gets smaller.

9. If a person's temperature is 92.8° it means that

    A. they are too cold.

    B. they are too hot.

    C. they are at normal temperature.

    D. they have just eaten a big lunch.

10. If a person's temperature is 102° you might

    A. wrap them in a space blanket.

    B. put ice packs on them.

    C. place a butterfly strip on them.

    D. put on gloves so you don't make them any hotter.

Test C   Name: _____

Directions: Read the passage called "Produce." Then answer questions 11–20.

Produce

The part of the supermarket that you usually see first is called Produce. This part of the store is close to the front where you come in. In the produce section you can get fresh fruits and vegetables. You can also buy cut flowers. This part of the store is full of many colors and good smells!

Fruits

In Produce, things are placed in a way that makes them easy to find. There is an apple section. In that part you can choose from different kinds of apples. Some apples are dark red. Other apples are green. There are apples that are good for baking. Others are good to have as a snack in your lunch.

You can find citrus fruits in Produce. Citrus fruits are a type of fruit that grow on trees. They are easy to peel. Citrus fruits have seeds. Lemons are citrus fruits. So are limes and grapefruits. The most popular kind of citrus fruit is the orange. Oranges taste great. They are good for you. Some oranges have seeds, but there are kinds that are seedless.

Not all fruits in Produce cost the same amount of money. You will see a sign in front of every fruit that tells you how much it costs. Sometimes you can buy a certain amount of fruit for a dollar. You may get three limes for one dollar. Some fruit is sold by the pound.

There are scales in the store. People put their fruit in plastic bags. Then they weigh it on the scale. This gives you an idea of how much the fruit will cost when you get to the checkout line.

People love to eat bananas. In the store you will see a huge place where all of the bananas are. Bananas come in a bunch. Some bunches can have as many as 10 bananas on them. If you don't want 10, you just break apart the amount you do want. The trick to picking a good banana is its color. If it is too green it means that it is not ripe. It will not taste so great. If it is black it means that it is too ripe. It will taste mushy and bland.

There are lots of other fruits you can buy in the produce area. Large melons, different types of berries, and grapes can all be found in this area.

| **Test C** | **Name:** _____ |

Produce *(cont.)*

Vegetables

There are vegetables in the produce section, too. They are set up in ways that make it easy for people to find what they want.

One thing you can buy is leafy greens. Spinach is a leafy green. So are kale and collards. Leafy greens can be sold in a bunch held together with a twist tie. Sometimes they are sold in plastic bags.

The vegetables in the produce section come in all kinds of strange shapes. Think about tasty mushrooms. Some are white. They look like buttons. Others are dark brown. They are shaped like little umbrellas. You can buy mushrooms loose, or you can buy them in a tiny box.

There are some veggies that are shaped like medium-sized balls. These are called heads. You can get a head of iceberg lettuce or a head of red or white cabbage. Green broccoli and white cauliflower also come in heads.

Even though most grocery stores have much of the same produce, sometimes they can be very different. Let's say that you are in a store in a place that's warm and sunny all year long. That store will have more types of produce to choose from.

If you were in a place where it's very cold, you may see fewer kinds of fruits and vegetables.

That's Not All, Folks!

If you need to buy a gift, you might want to go to the produce part of a grocery store. You can get more than just fruits and vegetables there. You can buy fresh cut flowers. Most of the time the flowers come in bunches. Sometimes they come in pretty arrangements. Most of the flowers are kept in big buckets of water. They are also kept in a refrigerator to keep them fresh.

Meet the Produce Manager

Hi. My name is Bobby Roman. I am a produce manager at Shop-and-Save. My job is to make sure that the produce we sell is fresh. Every day, I go through all of the fruits and vegetables. I look for things that are too ripe or rotten. I throw those things away. Then I replace them with fresh produce. I also help customers. I teach them how to cook vegetables. I show them how to use their sense of smell to find out if something is just right. My job is fun. I take pride in my part of the store.

Name: _____

Produce *(cont.)*

Questions 11–20: Select the best answer.

11. What is produce?

    A. flowers

    B. canned fruit and vegetables

    C. fruits

    D. fruits and vegetables

12. Where is the produce in the store often located?

    A. near the frozen foods

    B. near the bread

    C. near the front of the store

    D. near the pet food

13. How are the fruits arranged?

    A. apples go with apples, oranges go with oranges

    B. all of the fruits are mixed together

    C. bananas go with citrus fruits

    D. rotten fruit goes together, ripe fruit goes together

14. Which one is not a citrus fruit?

    A. orange

    B. lime

    C. grapefruit

    D. peach

15. What does it mean if a banana is green?

    A. It is too ripe.

    B. It will be mushy.

    C. It is not ripe.

    D. It will taste good.

Test C   Name: _____

Produce *(cont.)*

16. What kind of vegetable is kale?

    A. a leafy green

    B. a cabbage

    C. a mushroom

    D. cauliflower

17. What vegetable is shaped like an umbrella?

    A. red cabbage

    B. mushroom

    C. carrot

    D. spinach

18. Which store would have the most kinds of produce?

    A. a store in Alaska

    B. a store in Colorado

    C. a store in New York

    D. a store in Florida

19. What would the produce manager do if he saw black bananas?

    A. throw them away

    B. eat them

    C. sell them for less money

    D. make banana bread

20. What else can you find in the produce part of the store?

    A. bread and cookies

    B. flowers

    C. meat

    D. birthday gifts

Test C   Name: _____

Directions: Read the passage called "U.S. Presidents." Then answer questions 21–30.

U.S. Presidents

The president is the head of our country. The United States has had 44 presidents. Some are well known. Some are not. Read to learn about some presidents you know and some presidents you may not have heard of before.

George Washington is a famous president. He is called the "Father of Our Country." He was our first president. George Washington was the president over two hundred years ago.

You see George Washington all the time. The face on the quarter in your pocket is George Washington. He is on the dollar, too. There are lots of things that are named for him. Our capital is named for him. There are parks and forts named for him. There are towns named for him.

Abraham Lincoln was our 16th president. He is also known as "Honest Abe." Lincoln was a brave president. He was the president who made slavery a crime. You see Lincoln all the time as well. He is on the penny. He is on the five-dollar bill. When you think of Abe, you may picture a man in a black stovepipe hat. Men wore those kinds of hats in his time.

Washington and Lincoln are on a famous monument. It is called Mount Rushmore. It is in South Dakota. It is a huge carving in the side of a mountain.

Not all presidents are famous. Take Benjamin Harrison. He was the 23rd president. He was president in the 1890s. When he was president, he spent one billion dollars. That was the first time the government spent that much money. Harrison did some cool things, too. He was the first president to record his voice. He was the first to go to a baseball game. Harrison put electricity in the White House.

Martin Van Buren was the 8th president. When he was in office the country had problems with money. Many people did not have jobs. They blamed Van Buren. Van Buren had a nickname. It was Old Kinderhook because he was born in Kinderhook, New York. Some people believe this is how we got the word "okay." The O stands for Old, and the K stands for Kinderhook. Van Buren was on the eight-cent stamp from 1938. Van Buren had big, bushy sideburns on his face. These were called "mutton chops."

Franklin Pierce was the 14th president. He was born in a log cabin. He is known for being handsome. He was the first president to put a Christmas tree in the White House. Pierce had a sleeve dog. A sleeve dog is so tiny it can fit into a tea cup. Pierce had a sad life. All of his children died when they were very young. They did not live to see their father become president.

Test C   Name: _____

U.S. Presidents *(cont.)*

Gerald Ford was the 38th president. Many people who are alive today will remember him. When Ford was young he worked as a fashion model. He was the first president whose parents were divorced. He loved to ski. He also had a chance to play football with the NFL. He had a golden retriever named Liberty. Ford lived to be very old. He died when he was 93.

If you were born after 2000 then there have only been a few presidents so far in your lifetime. Barack Obama is one and before him was George W. Bush. As you grow you will see many presidents come and go. Some of them will do things that you like. Others will not. Some will be well known after they are gone, but not all of them. It is hard to know now who might become as famous as George Washington. Only time will tell.

Questions 21–30: Select the best answer.

21. How many presidents are named in the passage?

   A. 8

   B. 6

   C. 10

   D. 44

22. Why is Washington called the "Father of Our Country"?

   A. He loved children.

   B. He is on the dollar bill.

   C. He was the first president.

   D. Many parks and schools are named for him.

23. What kind of hat did Lincoln wear?

   A. coonskin hat

   B. baseball hat

   C. cowboy hat

   D. stovepipe hat

24. Where is Mount Rushmore?

   A. North Dakota

   B. South Carolina

   C. South Dakota

   D. Washington, D.C.

Test C   Name: _____

U.S. Presidents *(cont.)*

25. Which president was the first to spend one billion dollars?

    A. Abe Lincoln
    B. Gerald Ford
    C. Barack Obama
    D. Benjamin Harrison

26. Where does the word *okay* come from?

    A. Van Buren's nickname
    B. the town of Kinderhook, New York
    C. Franklin Pierce
    D. bushy sideburns

27. Who was the first president to put up a Christmas tree in the White House?

    A. Benjamin Harrison
    B. Van Buren
    C. Pierce
    D. Obama

28. What is true about Gerald Ford?

    A. He was really good at sports.
    B. He was a great president.
    C. He is on the five dollar bill.
    D. He was the 43rd president.

29. Who was the president just before Barack Obama?

    A. Abe Lincoln
    B. Benjamin Harrison
    C. Gerald Ford
    D. George W. Bush

30. What do Pierce and Ford have in common?

    A. They both had dogs when they were president.
    B. They both had parents who were divorced.
    C. They were both on the 20-dollar bill.
    D. They both played football.

Test C   Name: _____

Directions: Read the interview. Then answer questions 31–40.

Ten Questions for Punxsutawney Phil

by News E. Jones for *The Furry Times*
March, GOBBLER'S KNOB, PA

Punxsutawney Phil is the most famous groundhog in the entire world. He predicts whether we will have six more weeks of winter, or if spring is on its way. He sat down with me recently for an exclusive interview. I was the only person to ask him questions.

Q. How did you get your job as the Groundhog Day groundhog?

A. It's a family business. My father had the job before me, and my grandfather before him, all the way back to my great-great-grandfather.

Q. You have a brother, Fred. Why didn't he get the job?

A. He was afraid of his shadow. You can't be scared of your shadow if you are going to do this job.

Q. Is there any jealousy?

A. Not anymore. He works as my manager. He's a good kid.

Q. So how do you prepare for February 2nd?

A. It's kind of a two-part thing. First, I practice going in and out of my burrow. You want to get out of there smooth-like. A good entrance is everything.

Q. Yes, I remember there was a situation… back in 2006?

A. You had to bring that up? Worst day of my life. Horrible! I was coming out of my burrow, all smooth, when boom, I tripped on a stick and fell over on my side! I still have nightmares about it.

Q. Did you see your shadow that year? Do you recall?

A. The only thing I saw that year was the inside of an ambulance!

Q. Sorry. So, you were talking about your preparation.

A. Right. Right. Once I get out of the burrow, I take a good look around myself. First, I look to my left. Then, I look to my right. I can usually tell right away if I can see my shadow, and if I do, boom, I give you six more big ones. Then, it's back to the burrow for me.

Q. We hate getting six more big ones.

A. It's nothing personal. A groundhog's got to do what a groundhog's got to do.

Q. And if you don't see your shadow?

A. Well, then what's the hurry? I eat a little grass; I pose for a few pictures, sign a couple of autographs.

Q. I understand that the squirrels are trying to get their own day? Do you care to comment?

A. Squirrels! Please! It'll never happen. They're all nuts!

Test C   Name: _____

Ten Questions for Punxsutawney Phil *(cont.)*

Questions 31–40: Select the best answer.

31. What type of passage is this?

    A. newspaper article

    B. chapter from a book

    C. recipe

    D. journal entry

32. Who is being interviewed?

    A. News E. Jones

    B. Fred

    C. Punxsutawney Phil

    D. squirrels

33. If an interview is *exclusive*, what does that mean?

    A. It is a short interview.

    B. It is a long interview.

    C. It is fiction.

    D. Phil can't be interviewed by anyone else.

34. What is Phil's job?

    A. He predicts the weather.

    B. He pays money for lost teeth.

    C. He signs autographs.

    D. He digs a burrow.

35. How do you know that this article is fiction?

    A. Interviews usually have more than 10 questions.

    B. There are no groundhogs named Punxsutawney Phil.

    C. Animals don't talk, so it would be impossible to interview them.

    D. Groundhog Day is February 3rd, not February 2nd.

Test C | **Name:** _____

Ten Questions for Punxsutawney Phil *(cont.)*

36. Where does the interview take place?

    A. in a burrow

    B. near Phil's shadow

    C. in Gobbler's Knob

    D. in an ambulance

37. What does Phil still have nightmares about?

    A. not seeing his shadow in 2006

    B. how jealous his brother Fred is

    C. the squirrels getting their own day

    D. tripping on a stick in 2006

38. What does Phil mean by "six more big ones"?

    A. six more weeks of winter

    B. six more days of winter

    C. six more months of winter

    D. spring is on its way

39. What happens if Phil doesn't see his shadow?

    A. We get six more weeks of winter.

    B. He runs back into his burrow.

    C. Spring is on its way.

    D. Phil wins a trophy.

40. How does Phil probably feel about squirrels?

    A. He likes them.

    B. He dislikes them.

    C. He respects them.

    D. He's afraid of them.

| Test C | Name: _____ |

Directions: Read the passage called "The Party Planner." Then answer questions 41–50.

The Party Planner

So your birthday's coming up in a few weeks and you want to throw a big party? That's great! But there's more to planning a party than just buying the cake and blowing out the candles. You have to think about all kinds of things. Who will you invite? What kinds of food will you serve?

The first thing you should do is pick a theme for your party. Maybe it will be a bowling party. Or perhaps you might like to go ice skating. Of course, you don't have to have a theme. Just getting together with friends and family can be fun.

Next, you will want to pick a date. It would be great if your party was on your birthday, but sometimes that can't happen. Try to pick a date that is either on your birthday or as close to your birthday as you can.

So you have the date. Now you will have to send out the invitations. You can email them or send them in the mail. First, make a list of the people you would like to come to your party. Plan your list carefully. Include all of your friends from school. Don't forget about your family. They will want to celebrate your birthday with you too!

It's time to plan what kind of food you would like to serve at your party. Hot dogs and hamburgers? Pizza? Finger foods? Will you make the food yourself, or will you have help? Whatever you decide, give yourself plenty of time, and don't forget the cake and candles!

A fun part of your party will be the entertainment. Some people like to have clowns. Others have magicians. You don't have to have any of those things. You can have a good time by just playing games like Twister® or having a dance contest.

Sometimes people get gifts and cards on their birthdays. Have a place to put these things. Set a time to open your gifts with your guests. Don't forget to thank them. This is the most important part of your party.

What would a birthday party be without a cake and a song? Make sure you have little plates to put the cake on. It is also a good idea to have some foil around so you can wrap cake for people to take home with them.

When the party is over, make sure to thank everyone for sharing your birthday. A birthday is always more fun when it is shared with good friends and a loving family!

Test C   Name: _____

The Party Planner *(cont.)*

Questions 41–50: Select the best answer.

41. What does this passage teach you how to do?

  A. take a test

  B. plan your birthday party

  C. bake a cake

  D. dance

42. What is the first thing you should do when you plan your party?

  A. send out the invitations

  B. bake the cake

  C. open your gifts

  D. pick a theme

43. Which of these is not an example of a theme for a birthday party?

  A. bowling

  B. laser tag

  C. ice skating

  D. the date of your birthday

44. When is the best day to have your party?

  A. on the weekend

  B. on a school night

  C. on your birthday

  D. close to your birthday

45. What do you do after you pick a date for the party?

  A. pick a theme

  B. send the invitations

  C. open the gifts

  D. make the food

Test C   Name: _____

The Party Planner *(cont.)*

46. Which game was mentioned in this passage?

   A. hula hoops

   B. Memory

   C. Checkers

   D. Twister®

47. Which of these is an example of birthday entertainment?

   A. karaoke

   B. cake and candles

   C. gifts

   D. invitations

48. Which of these does the author think is the most important thing about your party?

   A. singing "Happy Birthday to You"

   B. thanking your guests

   C. sending out the invitations

   D. making the food

49. According to the passage, why would you need to have foil around at your party?

   A. to wrap pieces of cake for people to take home

   B. to use as decorations

   C. to cover the food that has not been eaten

   D. all of these

50. The main idea of this passage is

   A. birthday parties are fun.

   B. birthday parties are not worth the trouble.

   C. there's a lot involved in planning a birthday party.

   D. thanking people is the most important thing about your party.

Name: _____ **Date** _____

Bubble Answer Sheet   Test _____

1. (A) (B) (C) (D)   18. (A) (B) (C) (D)   35. (A) (B) (C) (D)

2. (A) (B) (C) (D)   19. (A) (B) (C) (D)   36. (A) (B) (C) (D)

3. (A) (B) (C) (D)   20. (A) (B) (C) (D)   37. (A) (B) (C) (D)

4. (A) (B) (C) (D)   21. (A) (B) (C) (D)   38. (A) (B) (C) (D)

5. (A) (B) (C) (D)   22. (A) (B) (C) (D)   39. (A) (B) (C) (D)

6. (A) (B) (C) (D)   23. (A) (B) (C) (D)   40. (A) (B) (C) (D)

7. (A) (B) (C) (D)   24. (A) (B) (C) (D)   41. (A) (B) (C) (D)

8. (A) (B) (C) (D)   25. (A) (B) (C) (D)   42. (A) (B) (C) (D)

9. (A) (B) (C) (D)   26. (A) (B) (C) (D)   43. (A) (B) (C) (D)

10. (A) (B) (C) (D)   27. (A) (B) (C) (D)   44. (A) (B) (C) (D)

11. (A) (B) (C) (D)   28. (A) (B) (C) (D)   45. (A) (B) (C) (D)

12. (A) (B) (C) (D)   29. (A) (B) (C) (D)   46. (A) (B) (C) (D)

13. (A) (B) (C) (D)   30. (A) (B) (C) (D)   47. (A) (B) (C) (D)

14. (A) (B) (C) (D)   31. (A) (B) (C) (D)   48. (A) (B) (C) (D)

15. (A) (B) (C) (D)   32. (A) (B) (C) (D)   49. (A) (B) (C) (D)

16. (A) (B) (C) (D)   33. (A) (B) (C) (D)   50. (A) (B) (C) (D)

17. (A) (B) (C) (D)   34. (A) (B) (C) (D)

Master Answer Sheet for Tests A, B, C

Answers for Test A (pages 18–37)

1. B	6. B	11. A	16. D	21. C	26. B	31. A	36. B	41. B	46. C
2. D	7. C	12. C	17. A	22. A	27. A	32. B	37. A	42. C	47. B
3. B	8. A	13. B	18. C	23. A	28. D	33. C	38. C	43. A	48. A
4. C	9. D	14. C	19. A	24. C	29. C	34. A	39. D	44. D	49. D
5. A	10. A	15. A	20. D	25. C	30. B	35. A	40. D	45. A	50. B

Answers for Test B (pages 38–60)

1. A	6. A	11. B	16. D	21. C	26. D	31. B	36. B	41. B	46. C
2. C	7. D	12. B	17. D	22. C	27. A	32. B	37. D	42. D	47. A
3. D	8. C	13. C	18. C	23. B	28. C	33. C	38. B	43. A	48. B
4. C	9. B	14. C	19. A	24. D	29. D	34. D	39. A	44. D	49. C
5. B	10. A	15. C	20. A	25. A	30. A	35. D	40. D	45. A	50. D

Answers for Test C (pages 61–77)

1. C	6. B	11. D	16. A	21. A	26. A	31. A	36. C	41. B	46. D
2. A	7. A	12. C	17. B	22. C	27. C	32. C	37. D	42. D	47. A
3. D	8. D	13. A	18. D	23. D	28. A	33. D	38. A	43. D	48. B
4. B	9. A	14. D	19. A	24. C	29. D	34. A	39. C	44. C	49. A
5. C	10. B	15. C	20. B	25. D	30. A	35. C	40. B	45. B	50. C

Test A Answer Key

1. B	6. B	11. A	16. D	21. C	26. B	31. A	36. B	41. B	46. C
2. D	7. C	12. C	17. A	22. A	27. A	32. B	37. A	42. C	47. B
3. B	8. A	13. B	18. C	23. A	28. D	33. C	38. C	43. A	48. A
4. C	9. D	14. C	19. A	24. C	29. C	34. A	39. D	44. D	49. D
5. A	10. A	15. A	20. D	25. C	30. B	35. A	40. D	45. A	50. B

Explanations for Test A Answers
Robinson Crusoe (pages 18–22)

1. **Correct Answer: B** *(Author's Style, Narration)* **E**
   The narrator identifies himself in the first sentence of Chapter 1.
   Incorrect Answers:
   A. There is a sea captain in the story, but he is not the narrator.
   C. Robinson speaks about his mother, but she is not the narrator of the story.
   D. There is a shipmate in the story, but he is not the narrator of the story.

2. **Correct Answer: D** *(Character Development, Motivation)* **I**
   Robinson spent his childhood in a port city, watching ships come and go and daydreaming about their travels. This helped to shape his future.
   Incorrect Answers:
   A. There is nothing in the passage to suggest that Robinson's father was a sailor.
   B. Robinson does make some money from being a sailor, but this was not his initial motivation to become one.
   C. No one forced Robinson to become a sailor.

3. **Correct Answer: B** *(Character Development, Feelings)*
   Robinson often speaks of his desire to see the world and not spend his life in York.
   Incorrect Answers:
   A. There is no evidence to suggest that Robinson would feel angry staying in York.
   C. There is no evidence to suggest that Robinson would feel safe staying in York.
   D. There is no evidence to suggest that Robinson would feel excited to stay in York. In fact he would feel the opposite, bored.

4. **Correct Answer: C** *(Making Deductions)*
   Robinson speaks about his mother's warnings of the dangers of the sea and her sadness when she hears that he wants to become a sailor.
   Incorrect Answers:
   A. Robinson's mother never mentions money.
   B. Robinson's mother does not fear that her son will get bored at sea.
   D. Robinson's mother does not fear that he will not learn a trade.

5. **Correct Answer: A** *(Locating Details)* **E**
   Robinson tells the reader that he went to sea when he was 18 years old.
   Incorrect Answers:
   B. Robinson does not go to sea at the age of 81.
   C. Robinson does not go to sea when he is 21.
   D. Robinson does not go to sea when he is 16.

6. **Correct Answer: B** *(Locating Details)*
   Robinson describes his first storm at sea in Chapter 2.
   Incorrect Answers:
   A. The storm at sea is not discussed in Chapter 1.
   C. The storm at sea is not discussed in Chapter 3.
   D. The storm is discussed in Chapter 2 but not chapter 3, so this answer has to be discarded.

7. **Correct Answer: C** *(Making Deductions)*
   During the storm, Robinson says that if he survives the storm he will never set foot on another ship.
   Incorrect Answers:
   A. Robinson recalls the words of his mother, but he doesn't promise to write more often.
   B. Robinson says that he will go home to stay with his mother and father, not see the world.
   D. Robinson says nothing about complaining to the captain.

Explanations for Test A Answers *(cont.)*

Robinson Crusoe *(pages 18–22)* *(cont.)*

8. **Correct Answer: A** *(Recalling Details)* **E**
The passage states that Robinson's first voyage was to London, and his second was to Africa.
Incorrect Answers:
B. Robinson's first voyage was to London.
C. Robinson is from York; he does not sail there.
D. Robinson does say that he has sailed to South America, but not on his second voyage.

9. **Correct Answer: D** *(Locating Details)*
Robinson explicitly describes most of his voyages as being unpleasant and full of disappointment.
Incorrect Answers:
A. Robinson only describes some of his voyages as being happy and successful.
B. Robinson does not describe his voyages as being terrifying and hard.
C. Robinson does not describe his voyages as being long and dull.

10. **Correct Answer: A** *(Recalling Details)*
Robinson explains that he became both a sailor and a trader.
Incorrect Answers:
B. The captain does not pay Robinson a salary.
C. Robinson does not work at the ports where the ship docks.
D. There is nothing to suggest that Robinson is a con man or dishonest.

11. **Correct Answer: A** *(Locating Details)* **E**
At the end of Chapter 3, Robinson states that he is going to tell the story about what ended his sailing career.
Incorrect Answers:
B. There is nothing to suggest that the story will be about Robinson's return home.
C. There is no mention of Robinson having become a ship captain.
D. This answer has to be eliminated since Robinson tells the reader what he will tell them next.

The Big Snow *(pages 23–26)*

12. **Correct Answer: C** *(Recalling Details)* **E**
The passage states that the family moved from Florida to Vermont.
Incorrect Answers:
A. The family moves to Troy; they are not from Troy.
B. The family moves to Vermont; they are not from Vermont.
D. There is no mention of Nevada in the story.

13. **Correct Answer: B** *(Recalling Details)*
The story clearly states that the family moved because the mom, who is a doctor, got a new job in Troy.

Incorrect Answers:
A. There is nothing to suggest that the family did not like living in Florida.
C. The dad did not get a new job; the mother did.
D. There is nothing to suggest that the family moved because they always wanted to live where it was snowy.

14. **Correct Answer: C** *(Making Inferences)* **I**
Chip states that he was afraid and that he would miss his friends. Most people would feel scared if they were going to be in an unfamiliar situation with people they don't know.
Incorrect Answers:
A. There is nothing to suggest that Chip is moving to a rough neighborhood.
B. There is nothing to suggest that Chip is fearful of flying on a plane.
D. Chip is not afraid of snow; he is just unfamiliar with it.

15. **Correct Answer: A** *(Recalling Details)*
Chip is from Miami, Florida. He has never seen snow there.
Incorrect Answers:
B. There is nothing to suggest that Chip is ill and can't go outside in cold weather.
C. Chip is not from the desert.
D. Chip is not visually impaired.

16. **Correct Answer: D** *(Character Analysis, Making Inferences)* **I**
The first thing Chip does is get dressed and race outside to play in the snow. This is the behavior of a person who is excited.
Incorrect Answers:
A. If Chip were afraid of the snow, he wouldn't run out into it.
B. If the snow bored Chip, he would not race out to play in it.
C. If the snow disgusted Chip, he wouldn't be around it or touching it.

17. **Correct Answer: A** *(Locating Details)*
The story clearly states that Chip checks the weather report every day.
Incorrect Answers:
B. There is no mention of a bike in the story.
C. Chip checks the forecast in Troy, Vermont, not Florida.
D. Chip does not check his backyard every day.

18. **Correct Answer: C** *(Making Inferences)*
Chip's anticipation of the coming snow storm is keeping him awake at night.

Explanations for Test A Answers *(cont.)*

The Big Snow *(pages 23–26)* *(cont.)*

Incorrect Answers:

A. Worry can keep people awake, but this is not why Chip is awake and can't sleep.

B. Fear can keep people awake, but this is not what is keeping Chip awake.

D. Chip does not have a virus.

19. Correct Answer: A *(Recalling Details)* **E**

After a few minutes of playing in the snow, Chip tells the reader that he was soaked to the bone.

Incorrect Answers:

B. Chip did not get hurt by playing in the snow.

C. Chip did not get lost playing in the snow.

D. Chip did have a snowball fight with his parents, but this is not the first thing that happened.

20. Correct Answer: D *(Making Inferences)* **I**

Because Chip has no experience with playing in snow, he didn't realize how important it was to wear the right clothes.

Incorrect Answers:

A. There is nothing to suggest that Chip is stubborn.

B. In his excitement, Chip forgot about his new snow clothes.

C. This is not stated in the text.

21. Correct Answer: C *(Recalling Details)*

The story says that Connie comes by with raisins and a carrot for the eyes and nose.

Incorrect Answers:

A. Chip's mother was already there.

B. Chip's father was already there.

D. It is possible that Connie is a neighbor, but since the options offer the specific name of Connie, the best answer must be Connie.

22. Correct Answer: A *(Character Analysis)*

In the beginning of the story, Chips says that he is afraid to move from Florida. At the end of the story he tells his dad that he likes living in Vermont.

Incorrect Answers:

B. Chips says that he likes Vermont, and we can see that he is enjoying himself in the snow.

C. Chip does not mention Florida once he moves to Vermont.

D. The opposite of this option is true.

How to Make a Snowman *(pages 27–29)*

23. Correct Answer: A *(Locating Details)* **E**

The passage states that mushy snow is not good for making snowmen.

Incorrect Answers:

B. All snow is cold, so this option makes no sense.

C. The passage does not mention anything about icy snow.

D. If even one of the options is wrong then you cannot select *all of these*.

24. Correct Answer: C *(Making Inferences)* **I**

Because your fingers are separated it may give you more flexibility of movement in order to shape and smooth the snowballs.

Incorrect Answers:

A. Gloves are not warmer than mittens simply because they are gloves.

B. This is an opinion and has nothing to do with making a good snowman.

D. Mittens and gloves would get wet at the same rate depending on the material from which they are made.

25. Correct Answer: C *(Locating Details)*

The instructions state that the first ball that you make is used for the base of the snowman.

Incorrect Answers:

A. The second ball is used for the middle section.

B. The third ball is used for the head.

D. There is no fourth ball.

26. Correct Answer: B *(Recalling Details)*

Three balls are made: one for the base, one for the middle, and one for the head of the snowman.

Incorrect Answers:

A. Two is not what is stated in the text.

C. Four is too many.

D. One is not enough.

27. Correct Answer: A *(Locating Details)*

Step Five states that you put the middle ball on top of the bottom ball.

Incorrect Answers:

B. This option is illogical.

C. This is Step Six.

D. This is Step Nine.

28. Correct Answer: D *(Locating Details)*

Step Seven describes packing snow between each layer.

Incorrect Answers:

A. Step Eight describes making a face for the snowman.

B. Step Nine describes putting a hat and scarf on the snowman.

C. Step Six describes placing the small ball on top of the middle ball.

29. Correct Answer: C *(Making Deductions)* **I**

Licorice jelly beans are black. Black eyes on a white snowman would really stand out.

Incorrect Answers:

A. Cherry jelly beans are red. They would not stand out as well as black jelly beans. Red might look scary.

Explanations for Test A Answers (cont.)

How to Make a Snowman (pages 27–29) (cont.)

B. Vanilla jelly beans are white. These would blend in with the snowman because it is also white.

D. Lemon jelly beans are yellow. Tiny yellow jelly beans would not stand out as much as black on a white snowman.

30. **Correct Answer: B** (Making Deductions)
A banana is curved in an arc. A large yellow banana would show up on a snowman, and also make it look as if he is smiling.
Incorrect Answers:
A. Smelling good would not enhance the look of the snowman.
C. If birds ate the mouth, the snowman's face wouldn't last very long.
D. The fact that the banana won't melt is not relevant as eventually the snowman will.

31. **Correct Answer: A** (Locating Details) E
Step Nine states that the top hat is traditional.
Incorrect Answers:
B. There is no mention of a baseball cap.
C. There is no mention of a cowboy hat.
D. There is no mention of a straw hat.

Amazing Ants (pages 30–33)

32. **Correct Answer: B** (Author's Purpose) I
"Amazing" is an adjective that usually conveys admiration for someone or something. You can infer that if you admire something you would probably also respect it.
Incorrect Answers:
A. If the author feared ants, she may have used a number of other adjectives, like *fearsome, frightening,* or *creepy.*
C. Things that are described as being amazing are not necessarily cute.
D. The author may like ants, but the best choice in this case is B. It more accurately describes the author's opinion of ants.

33. **Correct Answer: C** (Locating Details) E
The passage clearly states that ants can be yellow, brown, red, or black.
Incorrect Answers:
A. Ants can be black, but not orange.
B. Ants can be red, but not tan.
D. You cannot select *all of these* if even one of the options is incorrect.

34. **Correct Answer: A** (Locating Details)
The passage states than an exoskeleton is like a hard shell.
Incorrect Answers:
B. An exoskeleton is like the bones on the inside of a human body, but it is not the same thing. It protects the organs from the outside.

C. "Exoskeleton" is not another word for feelers.

D. The exoskeleton is not the stinger of the ant.

35. **Correct Answer: A** (Interpreting Graphic Features, Diagram)
The diagram shows that the poison sac is located on the rear of the ant.
Incorrect Answers:
B. The feelers, eyes, and pinchers are located on the ant's head, according to the diagram.
C. The poison sac is not located on the tips of the ant's claws according to the diagram.
D. The poison sac is not located near the ant's eye.

36. **Correct Answer: B** (Locating Details)
The passage states that the feelers help an ant to smell.
Incorrect Answers:
A. The pinchers help the ant to fight and dig.
C. The claws do not help the ant to smell.
D. The exoskeleton is a hard shell that does not help the ant to smell.

37. **Correct Answer: A** (Locating Details)
The passage states that social animals are animals that live in groups.
Incorrect Answers:
B. Social animals live together, not alone.
C. Having an exoskeleton has nothing to do with whether an animal is social or not.
D. Some carnivorous animals may live in groups, others may not.

38. **Correct Answer: C** (Locating Details) E
The passage states that the worker ants defend the colony, get food, and build the nest.
Incorrect Answers:
A. The queen ant lays the eggs. She does not defend the colony. She is defended by the colony.
B. The male ant is responsible for fertilizing the eggs, not defending the colony.
D. It is true that the worker ants defend the colony, but not the queen or the males.

39. **Correct Answer: D** (Making Deductions)
Without the queen and the males the colony would not survive. They are more important to the colony than the worker ants. For this reason, it makes sense for them to have wings in order to escape from the kind of danger that the worker ants can't defend.
Incorrect Answers:
A. Generally, wings are not an adaptation intended to frighten predators.
B. Queen and male ants seldom leave the nest, so they would not need to fly into it.
C. Wings don't make ants more attractive to other ants.

Explanations for Test A Answers *(cont.)*

Amazing Ants *(pages 30–33) (cont.)*

40. Correct Answer: D *(Author's Purpose, Text Organization)* **I**
The author intentionally bolded certain words to draw attention to them to let the reader know that they are important to the understanding of the topic.
Incorrect Answers:
- **A.** It is true that the bolded words are important words to learn about ants.
- **B.** Bolded words are not used in this context so that the passage looks nicer.
- **C.** Words that are bolded are easier to find in a passage.

41. Correct Answer: B *(Locating Details)* **E**
The passage states that one way that ants help the environment is by tunneling in the soil, which allows air to enter into it. This keeps it fertile.
Incorrect Answers:
- **A.** Ants may eat garbage, but the passage does not say anything about this.
- **C.** Ants typically do not live inside of plastic containers, and if they did this would not be helpful to the environment.
- **D.** Some ants do live beneath mounds but this, in and of itself, is not helpful to the environment.

Jimmy's Big Barbecue Shack *(pages 34–37)*

42. Correct Answer: C *(Making Inferences)* **I**
The restaurant is called Jimmy's Big Barbecue Shack, so you can infer that the owner is named Jimmy. Many people name their businesses after themselves.
Incorrect Answers:
- **A.** It is unlikely that Jimmy is the name of someone's grandma since it is usually a male name.
- **B.** It is not impossible to say. There are clues in the restaurant's name to suggest an owner.
- **D.** In this instance, "shack" refers to a type of building, not a person's last name.

43. Correct Answer: A *(Locating Details)*
If you count the number of items listed under Combo Plates you will count five.
Incorrect Answers:
- **B.** There are six sandwiches, not six combo plates.
- **C.** There are 11 combo plates and sandwiches combined, but not 11 combo plates.
- **D.** There are 17 sandwiches, combo plates, and side dishes combined, not 17 combo plates.

44. Correct Answer: D *(Locating Details)*
The menu says that three ribs come with the Classic BBQ Sampler.
Incorrect Answers:
- **A.** Two ribs come with the Lunch Plate, not the Sampler.
- **B.** Four ribs come with the Rustling Rib Plate, not the Sampler.
- **C.** The Classic BBQ Sampler does not come with 12 ribs according to the text.

45. Correct Answer: A *(Making Deductions)*
A pulled-pork sandwich costs $6.00 and an additional fountain drink costs $1.50. Six dollars plus $1.50 equals $7.50.
Incorrect Answers:
- **B.** Six dollars is the cost of the sandwich by itself.
- **C.** One dollar and fifty cents is the cost of the additional fountain drink by itself.
- **D.** The cost is not eight dollars and fifty cents.

46. Correct Answer: C *(Making Deductions)* **I**
If something is famous, it usually means that it is also popular. You can then infer that the Famous Texas BBQ Beef is the most popular item on the menu.
Incorrect Answers:
- **A.** Jimmy may think it is the best item on the menu, but that is not stated in the next.
- **B.** Barbecued beef is a very common food item in many parts of the country, so it is not likely that Jimmy's is the only place where you can get this kind of beef.
- **D.** There are several items on the menu that cost $7.00, and they are not described as being famous.

47. Correct Answer: B *(Determining Meaning)*
The Grilled Portobello is described as "vegetarian friendly." Vegetarian means that it contains no meat.
Incorrect Answers:
- **A.** Beef is meat that comes from cows.
- **C.** The Lunch Plate contains spare ribs, which are meat.
- **D.** Italian sausage is made from pork, which is meat.

48. Correct Answer: A *(Locating Information)* **E**
The menu explains that the Lunch Plate comes with one side. Collard greens is the only side listed that is available at Jimmy's.
Incorrect Answers:
- **B.** Baked potato is not on the menu.
- **C.** Mac and cheese is not on the menu.
- **D.** Onion rings are not on the menu.

49. Correct Answer: D *(Determining Meaning)*
The side dishes come in different sizes. *Oz.* is the abbreviation for ounces, and *Qt.* is the standard abbreviation for quart.
Incorrect Answers:
- **A.** Qt. is not the abbreviation of quarter.
- **B.** Pt. is the abbreviation for pint, not quart.
- **C.** Qt. is not the abbreviation for quarter-pounder.

50. Correct Answer: B *(Determining Meaning)*
Daily means that the event occurs every day. If desserts are made every day, they will be fresh.
Incorrect Answers:
- **A.** This is not the meaning of daily.
- **C.** Weekly means once per week.
- **D.** This is not the meaning of daily. It is unlikely that a restaurant could make single slices of pie to order.

Test B Answer Key

1. A	6. A	11. B	16. D	21. C	26. D	31. B	36. B	41. B	46. C
2. C	7. D	12. B	17. D	22. C	27. A	32. B	37. D	42. D	47. A
3. D	8. C	13. C	18. C	23. B	28. C	33. C	38. B	43. A	48. B
4. C	9. B	14. C	19. A	24. D	29. D	34. D	39. A	44. D	49. C
5. B	10. A	15. C	20. A	25. A	30. A	35. D	40. D	45. A	50. D

Explanations for Test B Answers

Teeth (pages 38–43)

1. **Correct Answer: A** (Locating Information)
   The passage states that babies begin to get their first teeth when they are about 6 months old.
   Incorrect Answers:
   B. The passage states that by the time babies are 3, they have their first set of teeth, but 3 years of age is not when they begin to come in.
   C. At the age of 13, a person has his or her permanent teeth.
   D. Babies don't have any teeth for their first few months of life.

2. **Correct Answer: C** (Locating Information) E
   The passage states that the first set of are called primary teeth. The prefix prim or prime means first.
   Incorrect Answers:
   A. Permanent teeth are the second set of teeth that come in.
   B. "Firsties" is a made-up term.
   D. "Premolars" is the name of a single type of tooth.

3. **Correct Answer: D** (Locating Details)
   The passage states that there are 20 teeth in a set of primary teeth.
   Incorrect Answers:
   A. There are 28 teeth in a set of permanent teeth.
   B. Eight is an incorrect answer according to the text.
   C. Twenty-five is an incorrect answer.

4. **Correct Answer: C** (Recalling Details)
   The passage states that you are 13 years old when you have your first set of permanent teeth.
   Incorrect Answers:
   A. You get your first set of primary teeth by the time you are 3, in most cases.
   B. Seventeen is an incorrect answer according to the text.
   D. Nineteen is an incorrect answer.

5. **Correct Answer: B** (Making Inferences) I
   The passage says that you get wisdom teeth when you are about 18 years old. They are the last teeth you get. You can infer that these are called wisdom teeth because wisdom is usually associated with being older.
   Incorrect Answers:
   A. There is no mention of a Dr. Wisdom in the passage.
   C. Wisdom teeth do not make you smarter.
   D. Some people have them removed if they are causing problems, but this has nothing to do with why they are called wisdom teeth.

6. **Correct Answer: A** (Locating Information)
   The passage states that you have incisors, canines, molars, and premolars—four different types of teeth.
   Incorrect Answers:
   B. You have 28 permanent teeth, not 28 different types of teeth.
   C. There are 20 teeth in the primary set of teeth, not 20 different types of teeth.
   D. If you add 28 permanent teeth plus 4 wisdom teeth you would get 32, but there are not 32 different types of teeth.

7. **Correct Answer: D** (Using Word Reference Materials, Glossary)
   The glossary defines pulp as being where the nerves of the tooth are located.
   Incorrect Answers:
   A. The nerves are not located in the crown.
   B. The nerves are located in the pulp. The pulp is located in the cementum.
   C. The nerves are not in the jawbone.

Explanations for Test B Answers *(cont.)*

Teeth *(pages 38–43)* *(cont.)*

8. Correct Answer: C *(Locating Information)* **E**
The passage states that your premolars are located next to your canines.
Incorrect Answers:
- **A.** The canines are next to the incisors, not your premolars.
- **B.** Premolars are in front of molars.
- **D.** The wisdom teeth are the last teeth in your mouth. There are no teeth behind them.

9. Correct Answer: B *(Making Inferences)* **I**
The passage tells us that the canines are sharp and pointy and good for tearing food apart. Some foods don't need to be torn apart, but others, like a piece of steak, would need to be.
Incorrect Answers:
- **A.** The incisors, not the canines, would come in handy while eating a slice of pizza as it has to be cut into.
- **C.** The incisors, not the canines, would come in handy while eating corn on the cob as the kernels have to be cut away from the cob.
- **D.** You really don't need teeth to eat ice cream.

10. Correct Answer: A *(Making Inferences)* **I**
If you only ate fruits and vegetables you would use your molars the most to grind and mash the food.
Incorrect Answers:
- **B.** Incisors may be used for some types of fruit and vegetables, but not for most.
- **C.** The texture of most fruit and vegetables would not require the tearing and shredding of the canines.
- **D.** Wisdom teeth are specific kinds of molars, and this question requires a more general answer. If you selected wisdom teeth, it would mean that you would only use these teeth and not the other molars.

11. Correct Answer: B *(Using Word Reference Materials, Glossary)*
The words in any glossary are arranged alphabetically.
Incorrect Answers:
- **A.** The words are not arranged by order of importance. All of the words are equally important.
- **C.** The words are not arranged by which tooth part is the most sensitive.
- **D.** There is an order. If the words were random it would be very difficult for the reader to use this glossary.

The Owl and the Pussycat *(pages 44–46)*

12. Correct Answer: B *(Locating Details)*
The second line of the poem describes the boat as being pea-green.
Incorrect Answers:
- **A.** The owl and the pussycat take honey with them, but the boat is not honey-colored.
- **C.** The boat is not pink.
- **D.** The boat is not red.

13. Correct Answer: C *(Locating Details)* **E**
The poem states that Owl sang to a small guitar.
Incorrect Answers:
- **A.** The pig does not play the guitar. He sells them the ring.
- **C.** The pussycat does not play the guitar.
- **D.** The turkey does not play the guitar. He marries them.

14. Correct Answer: C *(Identifying Genre, Fantasy)*
The poem is fantasy, as many parts of it could never happen in real life; for instance, animals talking or sailing a boat.
Incorrect Answers:
- **A.** The poem is the opposite of realistic.
- **B.** The poem is not science fiction.
- **D.** The poem is not a fable. There is not a lesson to learn.

15. Correct Answer: C *(Character Analysis)*
Owl and Pussycat want to get married.
Incorrect Answers:
- **A.** There is no mention of a party.
- **B.** They already are sailing.
- **D.** The owl already does sing songs.

16. Correct Answer: D *(Locating Details)*
In the first stanza, the poem says that the owl and the pussycat took "honey and plenty of money."
Incorrect Answers:
- **A.** The poem does not mention clean clothes.
- **B.** The poem does not mention fancy clothes.
- **C.** Their boat is pea-green, but they don't take peas with them.

17. Correct Answer: D *(Vocabulary, Homophones)*
The words *fowl* and *ring* are both homophones. *Fowl* is a general term for bird. *Foul* means to do something wrong, or to spoil something. *Ring* is jewelry you usually wear on your finger. *Wring* is to twist something.
Incorrect Answers:
- **A.** "Ring" is a homophone, but it is not the only one in the second stanza.
- **B.** "Fowl" is a homophone, but it is not the only one in the second stanza.
- **C.** "Stood" is not a homophone.

Explanations for Test B Answers *(cont.)*

The Owl and the Pussycat *(pages 44–46)* *(cont.)*

18. Correct Answer: C *(Recalling Details)* **E**
The poem says that they bought the pig's nose ring.
Incorrect Answers:
- **A.** The turkey does not have a ring.
- **B.** They don't bring a ring with them.
- **D.** The ring is not under the Bong-Tree.

19. Correct Answer: A *(Determining Meaning, Context Clues)*
The line in which the word is located is "Dear pig, are you willing to sell for one shilling. . ." Usually, things are sold for money. A shilling is money in England.
Incorrect Answers:
- **B.** A shilling is not a guitar.
- **C.** A shilling is not a moon.
- **D.** A shilling is not a spoon.

20. Correct Answer: A *(Making Inferences)* **I**
The poem says that the owl and the pussycat danced "hand in hand, on the edge of the sand." Sand is usually located on a beach. Also, the owl and the pussycat arrived at their current location by boat, so that also suggests that they are on a beach.
Incorrect Answers:
- **B.** There is nothing to infer that the owl and the pussycat are on their boat at this point in the poem.
- **C.** The turkey lives on the hill, but that is not where they are at this point in the poem.
- **D.** There is enough information to take a good guess at where they are.

21. Correct Answer: C *(Making Deductions)* **I**
Cats usually prey on birds.
Incorrect Answers:
- **A.** Birds don't like each other the way people do.
- **B.** Animals don't like each other the way people do.
- **D.** Cats and owls don't dance at all.

America's National Monuments *(pages 47–50)*

22. Correct Answer: C *(Locating Information)*
The passage defines a national monument as being a place or a building that honors a person, an idea, or an event.
Incorrect Answers:
- **A.** Monuments are special places for Americans to visit, but this is not the definition of a monument.
- **B.** The Statue of Liberty is one of many national monuments.
- **D.** Some national monuments stands for freedom and hope, but this is not the definition of a national monument.

23. Correct Answer: B *(Locating Details)* **E**
The passage states that there are 101 national monuments in the United States.
Incorrect Answers:
- **A.** Fifty is not the correct answer.
- **C.** Ten is not the correct answer.
- **D.** One hundred sixty-one is not the correct answer.

24. Correct Answer: D *(Organization of Text, Alphabetical Order)*
The monuments are arranged in alphabetical order.
Incorrect Answers:
- **A.** The author's personal likes or dislikes are not suggested as to how the monuments are organized in the text.
- **B.** All of the monuments are equally important.
- **C.** The number of people who visit each monument is not how they are ordered in the text.

25. Correct Answer: A *(Text Organization, Lists)*
The date refers to the year that it was established as a monument.
Incorrect Answers:
- **B.** Some monuments were "discovered" and others were built.
- **C.** Not all of the monuments were built. Some are natural.
- **D.** You cannot select *none of these* if at least one of the options is correct.

26. Correct Answer: D *(Making Deductions)*
Devil's Tower is a landform that was created by natural forces like earthquakes, erosion, and volcanoes. It was not made by people.
Incorrect Answers:
- **A.** Fort McHenry was made by people.
- **B.** Booker T. Washington Monument is part of a house, and houses are made by people.
- **C.** Navajo was made by the ancient Anasazi people.

27. Correct Answer: A *(Locating Details)* **E**
The entry states that Fort McHenry is located in the state of Maryland.
Incorrect Answers:
- **B.** Booker T. Washington and George Washington Birthplace monuments are located in Virginia.
- **C.** There are no U.S. national monuments in Britain.
- **D.** The Statue of Liberty is located in New York Harbor.

Explanations for Test B Answers *(cont.)*

America's National Monuments *(pages 47–50)*
(cont.)

28. Correct Answer: C *(Locating Information)*
The entry for Navajo states that it is the location of the cliff dwellings of the ancient Anasazi.
Incorrect Answers:
- **A.** The passage says that Devil's Tower was a holy place for Native Americans, but not Navajo.
- **B.** Fort McHenry is the site of a famous battle, not Navajo.
- **D.** The passage does not discuss ancient drawings on rocks in the desert.

29. Correct Answer: D *(Making Deductions)* **I**
You can deduce, based on the other entries, including the Booker T. Washington and George Washington Monuments, that the home of George Washington Carver is the most likely option listed that is a national monument.
Incorrect Answers:
- **A.** Disney World is a fun place for visitors but does not have the same importance as a national monument.
- **B.** President Obama's childhood home may be a national monument one day, but probably not during his lifetime.
- **C.** The first car made in America may be in a museum somewhere, but things are usually not monuments.

30. Correct Answer: A *(Making Inferences)*
We make certain things monuments because they say something about our history and what we think is important. These places represent us.
Incorrect Answers:
- **B.** While monuments are interesting places to visit, this is not the meaning of the sentence "They stand for who we are."
- **C.** Having monuments does not make us a country.
- **D.** Some events and people are more important than others, but this is not the meaning of the sentence.

Three Swinging Pigs and a Wolf *(pages 51–56)*

31. Correct Answer: B *(Identifying Genre)*
The story is a fairy tale. The "Once upon a time…" is a clear indication.
Incorrect Answers:
- **A.** Fables typically do not start with the words "Once upon a time , , ," though they do end with a lesson such as helping one another.
- **C.** The story is fiction, but a more specific option is available, so you must select that one. You are looking for the best answer.
- **D.** Nonfiction means factual. This story couldn't possibly be factual.

32. Correct Answer: B *(Locating Details to Support Conclusions)*
The reader can infer from the fact that the pigs live together and have rhyming names that they are brothers. Additionally, the author refers to one as being "the runt of the litter." If they were all in the same litter they were related, not just friends.
Incorrect Answers:
- **A.** They may also be friends, but their primary relationship is as brothers.
- **C.** They are not neighbors. They live together in the same house.
- **D.** The pigs are boys, so they can't be sisters. The author uses the pronoun "he" to refer to them.

33. Correct Answer: C *(Drawing Conclusions)* **I**
The three pigs have names that rhyme. You can deduce that if there were a fourth pig, his name would also rhyme. Link is the only option that rhymes with Pink, Dink, and Stink.
Incorrect Answers:
- **A.** Jeb does not rhyme with the names of the pigs.
- **B.** Lucky does not rhyme with the names of the pigs.
- **D.** Curley does not rhyme with the names of the pigs.

34. Correct Answer: D *(Story Elements, Problem)*
Because the pigs have short legs, they can't get any momentum or height going when they try to swing themselves. One pig always has to push the others, so they can never swing together.
Incorrect Answers:
- **A.** The wolf threatens to blow their house down, but this is not the problem in the story.
- **B.** This is false. Mrs. Badger actually helps the pigs on the swings at one point in the story.
- **C.** Mr. Raccoon is unsuccessful at helping the pigs, but this is not the cause of the problem.

35. Correct Answer: D *(Character Analysis)* **I**
Mrs. Badger is always making sure that people obey the rules of the town. Telling people what to do is a trait of a bossy person.
Incorrect Answers:
- **A.** Nothing in the story suggests that Mrs. Badger is sweet.
- **B.** Nothing in the story suggests that Mrs. Badger is lazy.
- **C.** Nothing in the story suggests that Mrs. Badger is mean.

36. Correct Answer: B *(Interpreting Fiction, Plot)*
The thing that Mr. Raccoon builds is described as a crank, attached to a pulley, fixed to a stationary bike.
Incorrect Answers:
- **A.** There is no giant fan in the story.
- **C.** There are no levers that lift and drop the swings.
- **D.** Mr. Raccoon does not push the pigs with a giant broom.

Explanations for Test B Answers *(cont.)*

Three Swinging Pigs and a Wolf *(pages 51–56)* *(cont.)*

37. Correct Answer: D *(Character Analysis)*
The pigs explain to the wolf that he doesn't have any friends because all he does is blow houses down and that doing so is mean.
Incorrect Answers:
A. The pigs do not offer the wolf any money.
B. The pigs do not threaten to call Mrs. Badger.
C. The pigs do not say they will allow the wolf to blow down part of their house.

38. Correct Answer: B *(Locating Details)*
The pigs tell the wolf that he can't think for himself.
Incorrect Answers:
A. The pigs know the wolf is not nice, but that is not what the pigs say he can't do.
C. The pigs do not say that the wolf can't blow their house down. They know that he can.
D. The pigs talk about the fact that he can't make friends when he is being mean.

39. Correct Answer: A *(Story Elements, Solution)*
The wolf is able to blow on the backs of all three pigs at the same time so they can swing together.
Incorrect Answers:
B. The wolf does not use his legs to push the pigs.
C. The wolf does not build a machine called the Pigswinger.
D. The wolf does not get some of his friends to help.

40. Correct Answer: D *(Story Elements, Theme)* I
The wolf is able to use his natural talents to help instead of harm. Other characters also help one another. This is the theme of the story.
Incorrect Answers:
A. Friendship is important, but this is not the main theme of the story.
B. Bravery is not the theme of the story.
C. The pigs do solve their problem together, but this not the main theme of the story.

All About Pasta *(pages 57–60)*

41. Correct Answer: B *(Locating Details)* E
The first line of the second paragraph states that pasta comes from Italy.
Incorrect Answers:
A. Pasta is eaten in the United States, but it did not originate here.
C. Pasta is technically from Europe, but because Italy is an option you should select it because it is the best (more specific) answer.
D. Noodles are eaten in China, but pasta is not from there.

42. Correct Answer: D *(Locating Information)*
The passage states that a staple food is a food that you can eat almost every day.
Incorrect Answers:
A. Usually people only eat desserts occasionally, and a staple food is eaten almost daily.
B. Staple foods are not special holiday foods.
C. Staple foods are typically healthy, but that is not the definition of a staple item.

43. Correct Answer: A *(Making Deductions)* I
Bread is something that most Americans eat at least once a day; therefore, it is a staple food.
Incorrect Answers:
B. Most Americans do not eat ice cream every day; therefore it would not be considered a staple food.
C. Broccoli is not something that most Americans eat every day; therefore it is not a staple food.
D. Water is something that Americans have every day, but it is not a food.

44. Correct Answer: D *(Locating Information)*
Milk is not used in the making of pasta, so adding it would not be a step.
Incorrect Answers:
A. Adding salt is a step in the making of pasta.
B. Kneading the dough is a step in the making of pasta.
C. Adding the eggs is a step in the making of pasta.

45. Correct Answer: A *(Drawing Conclusions)*
Both capellini and spaghetti are long and kind of thin.
Incorrect Answers:
B. Penne is much shorter and thicker than capellini.
C. Farfalle is shaped like a butterfly, so it looks nothing like capellini.
D. Rotelle are shaped like little wheels, so they look nothing like capellini.

Explanations for Test B Answers *(cont.)*

All About Pasta (pages 57–60) (cont.)

46. Correct Answer: C *(Locating Information)*
Gomito are shaped like elbows. In fact, "gomito" means "elbow" in Italian.
Incorrect Answers:
- **A.** Rigatoni looks like short, fat tubes.
- **B.** Farfalle looks like bow ties or butterflies.
- **D.** Lumaconi looks like the shell of a large snail.

47. Correct Answer: A *(Making Deductions)* I
Lumaconi is the largest pasta listed in the options; therefore, you can deduce that it would take the longest to cook.
Incorrect Answers:
- **B.** Gomito are tiny elbow macaronis. They would not take long to cook.
- **C.** Penne are medium-sized. They would not take as long to cook as lumaconi.
- **D.** Rotelle are small, so they would not take as long to cook as lumaconi.

48. Correct Answer: B *(Locating Details)*
The directions state that you add salt to the boiling water.
Incorrect Answers:
- **A.** You do not use sugar when you are boiling the pasta.
- **C.** You do not use pepper when you are boiling the pasta.
- **D.** You do not add cheese when you are boiling the pasta.

49. Correct Answer: C *(Making Deductions)*
In order to twirl pasta, it has to be long and skinny. Capellini is the only option that fits this description.
Incorrect Answers:
- **A.** Farfelle is butterfly-shaped; it is not good for twirling.
- **B.** Penne is shaped like a small tube; it is not good for twirling.
- **D.** Rotelle is shaped like a wheel; it is not good for twirling.

50. Correct Answer: D *(Locating Information)*
The directions say that the pasta is ready when it is soft on the outside and a little hard on the inside.
Incorrect Answers:
- **A.** If the pasta is mushy it would mean that it was overcooked.
- **B.** The temperature of the pasta is not related to whether it is cooked or not.
- **C.** If the pasta is crunchy it would mean that was undercooked.

Test C Answer Key

1. C	6. B	11. D	16. A	21. A	26. A	31. A	36. C	41. B	46. D
2. A	7. A	12. C	17. B	22. C	27. C	32. C	37. D	42. D	47. A
3. D	8. D	13. A	18. D	23. D	28. A	33. D	38. A	43. D	48. B
4. B	9. A	14. D	19. A	24. C	29. D	34. A	39. C	44. C	49. A
5. C	10. B	15. C	20. B	25. D	30. A	35. C	40. B	45. B	50. C

Explanations for Test C Answers
The First Aid Kit (pages 61–64)

1. **Correct Answer: C** (*Making Deductions*)
    If someone gets hurt in a mall, then you can deduce that they are probably not near a hospital or a doctor.
    Incorrect Answers:
    A. You would not need a first aid kit in a hospital, because a hospital would already have everything required to help an injured person.
    B. You would not need a first aid kit in a doctor's office because it is likely that a doctor's office would already have most of what is required to help an injured person.
    D. You cannot select *none of these* if a least one of the other options is correct.

2. **Correct Answer: A** (*Locating Details*)
    The passage states that first aid kits usually have either a red or white cross on the outside.
    Incorrect Answers:
    B. The cross will not be on the inside. It has to be on the outside so people know it is a first aid kit.
    C. Some first aid kits are metal, but that's not how you can tell it's a first aid kit.
    D. Some first aid kits are made of cloth, but that's not how you can tell it's a first aid kit.

3. **Correct Answer: D** (*Locating Information*)
    The passage states the gloves are thrown away after use.
    Incorrect Answers:
    A. The gloves are not reused, so you would not put them back into the first aid kit.
    B. The gloves are thrown away, not put back into the box, whether they are turned inside out or not.
    C. There would be no reason to give the gloves to the person that you helped.

4. **Correct Answer: B** (*Comparing and Contrasting*)
    The passage states that a butterfly strip pulls the skin together to try to close a deep cut or wound.
    Incorrect Answers:
    A. The size is not what distinguishes a butterfly strip from a regular Band-Aid.
    C. Pulling the skin apart is the opposite of what a butterfly strip does.
    D. A butterfly strip is not used for burns.

5. **Correct Answer: C** (*Locating Information*)
    The passage states that an antiseptic is a liquid that kills germs.
    Incorrect Answers:
    A. An antiseptic is not a type of glove.
    B. An antiseptic is not something that is only used on burns.
    D. An antiseptic is not a bar of soap.

6. **Correct Answer: B** (*Making Deductions*)
    The passage states that the space blanket is made from a material that looks like foil. Foil is silver.
    Incorrect Answers:
    A. Red is not the color of foil.
    C. Purple is not the color of foil.
    D. Pink is not the color of foil.

7. **Correct Answer: A** (*Making Deductions*)
    The passage states that the space blanket is used by astronauts. Astronauts work in space, so you can deduce that this is how it got its name.
    Incorrect Answers:
    B. The blanket may not take up that much space, but that is not how it got its name.
    C. The space blanket is lightweight, but that is not how it got its name.
    D. The space blanket was not invented by a woman whose name is Space.

Explanations for Test C Answers *(cont.)*

The First Aid Kit *(pages 61–64)* *(cont.)*

8. **Correct Answer: D** *(Locating Information)*
   The passage states that the pupil gets smaller when a light is shined on it.
   Incorrect Answers:
   A. The pupil does not get larger when the penlight is shined on it.
   B. The eye may close, but it would be held open by the person using the penlight to see if the pupil gets smaller.
   C. The eye may be held open, but it does not open if the penlight is shined on it.

9. **Correct Answer: A** *(Making Deductions)*
   The passage states that normal body temperature is 98.6°, so if someone was 92.8° they would be too cold.
   Incorrect Answers:
   B. A person's temperature would have to be above 98.6° for them to be too hot.
   C. A temperature of 92.8° is not normal.
   D. How much a person has eaten does not have much to do with their body temperature.

10. **Correct Answer: B** *(Locating Information)*
    The passage states that if a person's temperature were 102°, which would be a high temperature, you could put ice packs on them to try to cool them down.
    Incorrect Answers:
    A. Wrapping them in a space blanket would be the opposite of what you should do.
    C. There would be no reason to use a butterfly strip unless he or she had a deep cut or wound.
    D. Wearing gloves would not affect the temperature of the person you are trying to help.

Produce *(pages 65–68)*

11. **Correct Answer: D** *(Determining Meaning)*
    The passage states that the produce section of the store is where you can get fresh fruits and vegetables, so you can determine that produce is fresh fruits and vegetables.
    Incorrect Answers:
    A. You can get flowers in the produce section, but flowers are not produce.
    B. To be considered produce, the fruits and vegetables must be fresh.
    C. Fruits are produce, but there is a more specific option here that should be selected because you are looking for the best answer.

12. **Correct Answer: C** *(Recalling Details)*
    The passage states that the produce section is near the front of the store where you come in.
    Incorrect Answers:
    A. The produce section is not near the frozen foods.
    B. The produce section is not near the bread.
    D. The produce section is not near the pet food.

13. **Correct Answer: A** *(Recalling Details)*
    The passage states that the produce is arranged so it is easy to find what you are looking for. The passage describes an apple section, a citrus section, etc.
    Incorrect Answers:
    B. If the fruits were all mixed together, it would be hard to find exactly what you were looking for.
    C. The passages say that the bananas have their own section. They don't go with the citrus fruits.
    D. Rotten fruit is thrown away, not displayed.

14. **Correct Answer: D** *(Making Deductions)*
    The passage states that citrus fruits grow on trees, are easy to peel, and have seeds. Oranges, lemons, limes, and grapefruits are identified as examples of citrus fruits, not peaches. You can deduce that a peach is not a citrus fruit because it has a pit instead of seeds.
    Incorrect Answers:
    A. An orange is a citrus fruit.
    B. A lime is a citrus fruit.
    C. A grapefruit is a citrus fruit.

15. **Correct Answer: C** *(Locating Information)*
    The passage states that if a banana is too green it means that it is not ripe.
    Incorrect Answers:
    A. A green banana is not too ripe. It is the opposite; it is not ripe enough.
    B. An overripe banana would be mushy.
    D. A green banana would not be ripe so it probably would not taste as good.

16. **Correct Answer: A** *(Making Information)*
    The passage states that kale is a leafy green.
    Incorrect Answers:
    B. A cabbage is not mentioned with the dark leafy vegetables.
    C. A mushroom is not a leafy green. It is white.
    D. Cauliflower is not a leafy green. It is white.

17. **Correct Answer: B** *(Locating Details)*
    The passage states that some mushrooms are shaped like little umbrellas.
    Incorrect Answers:
    A. Red cabbage is shaped like a head or a ball.
    C. Carrots are not mentioned in the passage at all.
    D. Spinach is a leafy green; it is not umbrella-shaped.

Explanations for Test C Answers *(cont.)*

Produce *(pages 65–68) (cont.)*

18. Correct Answer: D *(Making Deductions)*

The passage states that a grocery store located in a place that is warm and sunny most of the time will have a better selection than a store located in a cold place. The state of Florida is warm and sunny most of the time.

Incorrect Answers:

A. Alaska is warm and sunny sometimes, but a lot of the time it is very cold.

B. Colorado is sunny much of the time, and warm sometimes, but it can also be very cold.

C. New York state has four distinct seasons, and one of them (winter) can be very cold.

19. Correct Answer: A *(Making Deductions)*

The passage states that black bananas are overripe. The produce manager, Bobby Roman, says that part of his job is to throw rotten fruit away. You can deduce that because a black banana is nearly rotten, the produce manager would throw it away.

Incorrect Answers:

B. A black banana would not taste good, so it is not likely that the produce manager would want to eat it.

C. Most people would not want to buy black bananas no matter how cheap they were, so it is not likely that the produce manager would try to sell them for less.

D. It is not the job of the produce manager to bake bread.

20. Correct Answer: B *(Locating Details)*

The passage states that you can find fresh flowers in the produce section of the store.

Incorrect Answers:

A. Bread and cookies would be found in the bakery, not the produce section.

C. Meat is not kept in the produce section of the store.

D. Fresh flowers can be given as a birthday gift, but birthday gifts are not found in the produce section.

U.S. Presidents *(pages 69–71)*

21. Correct Answer: A *(Locating Information)*

If you count the names of all of the presidents mentioned in the story, you will count eight.

Incorrect Answers:

B. Six is an incorrect answer.

C. Ten is an incorrect answer.

D. There are 44 presidents, but only eight are mentioned.

22. Correct Answer: C *(Making Deductions)*

Washington is called the "Father of Our Country," as he was there right at its beginning.

Incorrect Answers:

A. Washington may have loved children, but this is not why he is called the "Father of Our Country."

B. Washington is on the dollar bill, but that is not why he is called the "Father of Our Country."

D. Many parks and schools are named after Washington, but that is not why he is called the "Father of Our Country."

23. Correct Answer: D *(Locating Details)*

The passage states that Lincoln wore a stovepipe hat.

Incorrect Answers:

A. Lincoln is not known for wearing a coonskin hat.

B. There were no baseball hats in Lincoln's time.

C. Lincoln was not known for wearing a cowboy hat.

24. Correct Answer: C *(Recalling Details)*

The passage states that Mount Rushmore is located in the state of South Dakota.

Incorrect Answers:

A. Mount Rushmore is not located in North Dakota.

B. Mount Rushmore is not located in South Carolina.

D. Mount Rushmore is not located in Washington, D.C.

25. Correct Answer: D *(Recalling Details)*

The passage states that Harrison was the first president to spend one billion dollars.

Incorrect Answers:

A. Abe Lincoln was not the first to spend one billion dollars.

B. Gerald Ford was not the first to spend one billion dollars.

C. Barack Obama was not the first to spend one billion dollars.

26. Correct Answer: A *(Locating Details)*

The passage states that Van Buren's nickname was *Old Kinderhook* as he was from the town of Kinderhook, New York. Old Kinderhook is probably where we got the word *okay* or the abbreviation *O.K.*

Incorrect Answers:

B. *Okay* comes from Van Buren's nickname, *not* the town of Kinderhook.

C. The word *okay* has nothing to do with Franklin Pierce.

D. Van Buren had bushy sideburns, but this is not where the word *okay* comes from.

Explanations for Test C Answers (cont.)

U.S. Presidents (pages 69–71) (cont.)

27. Correct Answer: C (Recalling Details)
The passage states that Pierce was the first president to have a Christmas Tree in the White House.

Incorrect Answers:
A. Benjamin Harrison was the first president to record his voice.
B. Van Buren was known for his "mutton chop" sideburns. There is no mention of Christmas in the passage about him.
D. Barack Obama is mentioned in the passage but no "firsts" are attributed to him.

28. Correct Answer: A (Making Deductions)
The passage states that Ford liked to ski and could have played football with the NFL. You can deduce that he was good at sports.

Incorrect Answers:
B. Whether or not Ford was a good president is not addressed in the passage.
C. Ford is not on the five-dollar bill, Lincoln is.
D. Ford was the 38th president. George W. Bush was the 43rd president.

29. Correct Answer: D (Locating Information)
The passage states that George W. Bush was the president before Barack Obama.

Incorrect Answers:
A. Abe Lincoln was president long before Barack Obama.
B. Benjamin Harrison was president long before Barack Obama.
C. Gerald Ford was president long before Barack Obama.

30. Correct Answer: A (Making Deductions)
The passage states that Franklin Pierce had a sleeve dog and Gerald Ford had a golden retriever.

Incorrect Answers:
B. Ford was the first president whose parents were divorced.
C. Neither one is on a 20-dollar bill.
D. Ford played football, Pierce did not.

Ten Questions for Punxsutawney Phil
(pages 72–74)

31. Correct Answer: A (Identifying Genre, Newspapers)
This passage is set up like a newspaper article. It has double columns and a byline. It also says the name of the newspaper, *The Furry Times*.

Incorrect Answers:
B. A chapter from a book would not have text set up in this manner.
C. A recipe would have a list of ingredients to make something to eat.
D. A journal entry would not be set up in this manner.

32. Correct Answer: C (Identifying Main Idea or Subject)
The title of the article is "Ten Questions for Punxsutawney Phil." The title makes it clear who is being interviewed.

Incorrect Answers:
A. News E. Jones is the one doing the interview, not the one being interviewed.
B. Fred is Phil's brother. He is not the subject of the interview.
D. Squirrels are mentioned in the interview, but they are not being interviewed.

33. Correct Answer: D (Determining Meaning)
If an interview is exclusive, it means that Phil agrees not to be interviewed by anyone else.

Incorrect Answers:
A. The interview is short, but the length of the interview has nothing to do with whether it is exclusive.
B. The fact that the interview is long has nothing to do with whether it is exclusive or not.
C. The interview is fiction, but that is not the meaning of "exclusive."

34. Correct Answer: A (Locating Information)
Phil is the name of the groundhog who works on Groundhog Day. The article states that it is his job to predict whether we will have six more weeks of winter, or whether spring is on its way.

Incorrect Answers:
B. The tooth fairy pays money for lost teeth, not Phil.
C. Phil does sign autographs, but that is not his only job.
D. Phil probably does dig his own burrow, but that is not his only job.

35. Correct Answer: C (Characteristics of Genre, Fiction)
An animal would never talk in real life, so this article must be fiction.

Incorrect Answers:
A. The number of questions does not determine whether the passage is fiction or not.
B. There is a groundhog named Punxsutawney Phil.
D. Groundhog Day is not on February 3rd. *When Groundhog Day is* has nothing to do with determining if the article is fiction or not.

36. Correct Answer: C (Locating Details)
You can see at the top of the article in the dateline that Phil was interviewed in March at Gobbler's Knob, PA.

Incorrect Answers:
A. Phil lives in a burrow, but it is unlikely he was interviewed in his burrow.
B. There is nothing to suggest that Phil was interviewed near his shadow.
D. Phil mentions that he was in an ambulance after an accident, but that is not where the interview takes place.

Explanations for Test C Answers *(cont.)*

Ten Questions for Punxsutawney Phil
(pages 72–74) *(cont.)*

37. Correct Answer: D *(Recalling Information)*
In the interview, Phil talks about tripping over a stick on Groundhog Day in 2006 and having to be taken away in an ambulance.
Incorrect Answers:
- **A.** Phil doesn't remember whether he saw his shadow or not, but that is not what gives him nightmares.
- **B.** Fred is jealous, but that is not what gives Phil nightmares.
- **C.** Phil is not happy that the squirrels want their own day, but that is not what gives him nightmares.

38. Correct Answer: A *(Idioms)*
"Six more big ones" is an expression that Phil uses to mean six more weeks of winter.
Incorrect Answers:
- **B.** "Six more big ones" does not mean six more days of winter.
- **C.** "Six more big ones" does not mean six more months of winter.
- **D.** "Six more big ones" does not mean that spring is on its way.

39. Correct Answer: C *(Making Inferences)*
The passage says that if Phil sees his shadow then we get six more weeks of winter. You can infer then that if Phil does not see his shadow then spring is on its way.
Incorrect Answers:
- **A.** We get six more weeks of winter if Phil *does* see his shadow.
- **B.** Phil does not run back into his burrow. He actually sticks around to eat grass and sign autographs.
- **D.** There is no mention of a trophy.

40. Correct Answer: B *(Character Analysis)*
Phil dismisses the idea that the squirrels should get their own day, saying they are nuts. It is more than likely that Phil dislikes the squirrels.
Incorrect Answers:
- **A.** Phil does not take the squirrels very seriously. This is not how you would act if you liked someone.
- **C.** Phil says that the squirrels are nuts. This is not a respectful thing to say.
- **D.** If Phil were afraid of the squirrels, he would not speak this way about them.

The Party Planner *(pages 75–77)*

41. Correct Answer: B *(Identifying the Main Idea)*
The passage is about everything that is involved in planning a birthday party.
Incorrect Answers:
- **A.** There is nothing in the passage about taking tests.
- **C.** Birthday cake is mentioned, but the passage is not about baking a cake.

- **D.** Dancing is mentioned, but the passage is not about dancing.

42. Correct Answer: D *(Locating Details)*
The passage states that picking a theme is the first thing that you should do.
Incorrect Answers:
- **A.** Sending out invitations is the third thing you should do, not the first.
- **B.** The passage does not say anything about baking a cake, just not forgetting about it.
- **C.** Opening your gifts is the sixth thing mentioned.

43. Correct Answer: D *(Making Deductions)*
The theme of the party would be similar to the idea or style of the party. Option D is the only option that is not a theme or idea.
Incorrect Answers:
- **A.** Bowling is a birthday party theme that was mentioned in the passage.
- **B.** Laser tag would be a theme for a birthday party.
- **C.** Ice skating is a birthday party theme that was mentioned in the passage.

44. Correct Answer: C *(Locating Details)*
The passage states that the best day on which to have your party would be the actual date of your birthday.
Incorrect Answers:
- **A.** The weekend might be a good time, but the question is asking you for the best day, which is the day of your actual birthday.
- **B.** A school night would probably not be the best time to have a party.
- **D.** A day close to your birthday might be a good time, but the question asks for the best time.

45. Correct Answer: B *(Text Organization, Steps in a Process)*
The passage states that after you pick a date for your party you send the invitations, which can either be emailed or mailed by the post office. This is the third thing you do.
Incorrect Answers:
- **A.** Picking a theme is the first thing you do.
- **C.** Opening the gifts is the sixth thing that you do.
- **D.** Making the food is the fourth thing you do.

46. Correct Answer: D *(Recalling Details)*
The passage mentions Twister®.
Incorrect Answers:
- **A.** Hula hoops are not mentioned in the passage.
- **B.** A memory game is not mentioned in the passage.
- **C.** Checkers are not mentioned in the passage.

Explanations for Test C Answers (cont.)

The Party Planner *(pages 75–77)* *(cont.)*

47. Correct Answer: A *(Making Deductions)*
Entertainment usually involves people or a set activity. Karaoke is a form of entertainment.
Incorrect Answers:
B. A cake and candles are not a form of entertainment.
C. Gifts are not a form of entertainment.
D. Invitations are not a form of entertainment.

48. Correct Answer: B *(Locating Information)*
The passage states that thanking your guests is the most important part of your party.
Incorrect Answers:
A. Singing a happy birthday song is a part of the party, but, according to the passage, not the most important part.
C. Sending out the invitations is important, but not as important as thanking your guests.
D. Making the food is also important, but not as important as thanking your guests.

49. Correct Answer: A *(Locating Information)*
The passage states that you can use foil to wrap pieces of birthday cake for guests to take home.
Incorrect Answers:
B. Foil is not used for the decorations.
C. Foil could be used to cover the food that has not been eaten, but the passage does not mention that.
D. You cannot choose *all of these* if even one of the options listed is incorrect.

50. Correct Answer: C *(Identifying the Main Idea)*
The passage is mostly about all of the things involved in planning a birthday party.
Incorrect Answers:
A. Birthday parties are fun, but this is not the main idea of the passage.
B. Birthday parties not being worth the trouble is not the main idea of the passage. All the planning would suggest that they are worth the trouble.
D. Thanking people is not the main idea of the passage.